MEMORY MANAGEMENT FOR DUMMIES™

Quick Reference

by Doug Lowe

IDG BOOKS

IDG Books Worldwide, Inc.
An International Data Group Company

Foster City, CA ♦ Chicago, IL ♦ Indianapolis, IN
Braintree, MA ♦ Dallas, TX

Memory Management For Dummies™ Quick Reference

Published by
IDG Books Worldwide, Inc.
An International Data Group Company
919 E. Hillsdale Blvd.
Suite 400
Foster City, CA 94404

Library of Congress Catalog Card No.: 94-74296

ISBN: 1-56884-362-3

Printed in the United States of America

10 9 8 7 6 5 4 3 2 1

1A/TQ/QR/ZV

Distributed in the United States by IDG Books Worldwide, Inc.

Distributed by Macmillan Canada for Canada; by Computer and Technical Books for the Caribbean Basin; by Contemporantea de Ediciones for Venezuela; by Distribuidora Cuspide for Argentina; by CITFC for Brazil; by Ediciones ZETA S.C.R. Ltda. for Peru; by Editorial Limusa SA for Mexico; by Transworld Publishers Limited in the United Kingdom and Europe; by Al-Maiman Publishers & Distributors for Suadi Arabia; by Simron Pty. Ltd. for South Africa; by IDC Communications (IIK) Ltd. for Hong Kong; by Toppan Company Ltd. for Japan; by Addison Wesley Publishing Company for Korea; by Longman Singapore Publisher Ltd. for Singapore, Malaysia, Thailand and Indonesia; by Unalis Corporation for Taiwan; by WS Computer Publishing Company, Inc. for the Philippines; by WoodsLane Enterprises Ltd. for New Zealand.

For general information on IDG Books in the U.S., including information on discounts and premiums, contact IDG Books at 800-434-3422 or 415-655-3000.

For information on where to purchase IDG Books outside the U.S., contact IDG Books International at 415-655-3021 or fax 415-655-3295.

For information on translations, contact Marc Jeffrey Mikulich, Director, Foreign & Subsidiary Rights, at IDG Books Worldwide, 415-655-3018 or fax 415-655-3295.

For sales inquiries and special prices for bulk quantities, write to the address above or call IDG Books Worldwide at 415-655-3000.

For information on using IDG Books in the classroom, or for ordering examination copies, contact Jim Kelly at 800-434-2086.

is a registered trademark of IDG Books Worldwide, Inc.

Acknowledgments

First of all, to Colleen Rainsberger: Thanks for keeping this project moving along, for improving the text at every turn, and for humoring me all the way through.

To Suzanne Packer and Jennifer Wallis: Thanks for your editorial prowess and attention to detail. Thanks also to Diane Giangrossi and Chuck Hutchinson for pitching in.

To Dennis Teague: Thanks for the thoroughness of your technical review and for all the great ideas I incorporated into the text.

To Mark Owens, Kathie Schnorr, and the rest of the production team: Thanks for the great layout and nifty icons.

To Diane Steele, Judi Taylor, Tracy Barr, and Sandra Blackthorn: Thanks for providing a great overall vision for this and all the ...*For Dummies* and *Quick Reference* books and for taking a chance on a somewhat different concept.

Finally, to Megg Bonar out here on the Left Coast: Thanks for getting this going, for the encouragement, and all the other stuff. Let's do it again!

Oh, and I would be remiss not to thank the original designers of the IBM PC, without whose 640KB memory limit this book would not have been possible (or necessary).

(The publisher would like to give special thanks to Patrick J. McGovern, without whom this book would not have been possible.)

ABOUT IDG BOOKS WORLDWIDE

WINNER
*Eighth Annual
Computer Press
Awards ⩾ 1992*

WINNER
*Ninth Annual
Computer Press
Awards ⩾ 1993*

IDG BOOKS

About the Author

Doug Lowe

Doug Lowe has written more than 15 computer books, including IDG's *Networking For Dummies* and *Powerpoint 4 For Windows For Dummies,* and knows how to present boring technostuff in a style that is both entertaining and enlightening. He is a contributing editor to IDG's *DOS Resource Guide.*

Credits

Executive Vice President, Strategic Product Planning and Research
David Solomon

Editorial Director
Diane Graves Steele

Acquisitions Editor
Megg Bonar

Brand Manager
Judith A. Taylor

Editorial Managers
Tracy L. Barr
Sandra Blackthorn
Kristin Cocks

Editorial Assistants
Tamara S. Castleman
Stacey Holden Prince
Kevin Spencer

Acquisitions Assistant
Suki Gear

Production Director
Beth Jenkins

Project Coordinator
Cindy L. Phipps

Pre-Press Coordinator
Steve Peake

Project Editor
Colleen Rainsberger

Editors
Diane Giangrossi
Suzanne Packer
Jennifer Wallis

Technical Reviewer
Dennis Teague

Production Staff
Paul Belcastro
Mark Owens
Carla Radzikinas
Dwight Ramsey
Patricia R. Reynolds
Kathie Schnorr
Gina Scott

Proofreader
Charles A. Hutchinson

Indexer
Steve Rath

Cover Design
Kavish + Kavish

Contents at a Glance

Introduction

Greetings! Welcome to *Memory Management For Dummies Quick Reference,* the memory management book that's less filling and looks great.

You've stumbled upon the ideal book if you want to improve your computer's use of memory but don't want to become an expert in anything remotely related to computers. This memory management book is for those of you who still have a life outside of the office and don't want to spend hours figuring out how to do things that should be easy.

This book does not teach you memory management from the ground up, as if memory management is a subject worth knowing something about. It's more of a "Help — I'm Out Of Memory!" book. It's for those panic-stricken moments when you get an error message that has something to do with memory and you're not sure how to deal with it.

Turn to this book when you want 30-Second-Right-Now-Don't-Waste-My-Time answers to your questions. You won't find pages and pages of tireless prose exploring all the subtle nuances of memory management. Instead, you'll get concise explanations of how to use what I think are the most important and useful memory management procedures. These procedures are designed to get you in and out of memory management as quickly as possible, because any time you spend futzing with memory management is time you could spend learning a foreign language, reading a good book, or doing any of those other things we're supposed to do in our spare time.

How to use this book

Keep this book within arm's reach of your computer. Whenever you're about to do something you're not 100 percent sure about, grab this book and look up what you're about to do to refresh your memory (and your computer's).

If you're new to memory management and have never made an attempt to optimize your computer's memory use, start by following the procedures described in Part I.

If you're *really* new to memory management and aren't sure of basic concepts, such as the difference between disk storage and computer memory, you may want to spend a few moments in Part VII, which explains the most important memory management buzzwords and jargon. Start by looking up *memory*, *RAM*, and *byte*. Skip around a bit with some of the other terms that catch your interest, but don't waste too much time. You can always return to Part VII when you come across a term you don't recognize.

I hate books that expect you to constantly flip from one section to another, so I've liberally interspersed definitions of key terms throughout the book as they come up. If a procedure deals with Upper Memory, for example, you'll find a brief definition of Upper Memory on the same page.

About MS-DOS Versions

This book assumes that you are using MS-DOS version 5.0 or any of the later MS-DOS versions, including 6.0, 6.2, 6.21, or 6.22. Unfortunately, versions of MS-DOS prior to 5.0 didn't include any memory management features, so the only way to improve memory management with those versions is to (1) use a third-party memory management program such as QEMM-386 or 386Max, or (2) upgrade to the current version of MS-DOS.

To find out what version of MS-DOS your computer is using, get to an MS-DOS command prompt and type the command **ver**.

What are all these parts?

This book is divided into seven parts:

Part I: Bare Bones Memory Management. This section contains the procedures you should follow the first time you attempt to optimize your computer memory. It includes procedures for finding out how much memory your computer has, removing unnecessary commands from your CONFIG.SYS and AUTOEXEC.BAT files, and running the MS-DOS 6 MemMaker command to optimize your computer's memory.

Part II: Common Memory Management Tasks. This section contains step-by-step procedures for the most common tasks of memory management. You'll find information on everything from running the MemMaker program to editing your CONFIG.SYS file to creating a configuration menu to support more than one memory configuration.

Part III: CONFIG.SYS and AUTOEXEC.BAT Files You Can Copy. This section contains a collection of CONFIG.SYS and AUTOEXEC.BAT files that can serve as models for your own. Feel free to copy these files and modify them to suit the individual needs of your computer.

Part IV: Memory Management Command Reference. This section contains detailed reference information about all of the MS-DOS commands that pertain to memory management.

Part V: Troubleshooting. This section provides help for the most common memory management panic situations. Turn to these pages if you get an error message that says something about not having enough memory or if your computer runs amok after you've made a change to your memory configuration.

Part VI. Adding Memory. This section summarizes the options for adding memory to 8088, 80286, and 386 or better systems, as well as the procedures for adding memory chips to your computer.

Part VII: Jargon and Buzzwords. This section explains the jargon and buzzwords you inevitably come up against when you deal with computer memory.

What all the pretty pictures mean

Just before this book went to the printer, we pelted it with a semi-automatic Icon assault rifle, now illegal in 17 states. As a result, this book is strewn with little pictures designed to convey information quickly. Here's the lowdown on the icons you'll find:

 This procedure is so easy that even an adult can do it.

 This procedure is a bit tricky. It isn't rocket science, but you should pay attention when using it to avoid potentially damaging mistakes.

 Clear your desk before attempting this operation. It requires your full attention from start to finish.

 If you mess this procedure up, nothing bad will happen.

 This procedure is easy enough, but if you mess it up you will get unwanted results.

 Messing up this procedure can cause you a lot of headaches. Find a guru to help you.

 Safe only in the hands of a programmer.

This feature requires MS-DOS 6 or a later version.

 This feature requires MS-DOS 6.2 or a later version.

 This feature requires MS-DOS 6.22 or a later version.

 This feature requires Windows 3.1.

 Be warned that this command consumes memory.

 It's time to reboot your computer (usually by pressing Ctrl-Alt-Delete).

 Watch out! Some technical drivel is just around the corner.

 This little tidbit of information can save you time and effort.

 Danger! Danger! Danger! You may be putting your files, your system, or yourself at risk if you don't heed these warnings.

 You can find more information about this topic elsewhere in this book.

 You can find more information about this topic in one of the other . . . *For Dummies* books.

Part I
Bare-Bones Memory Management

This part describes a two step procedure for memory management nirvana. It glosses over many of the subtleties of memory management in the interest of getting the job done quickly. In other words, this part is a bare-bones memory management procedure.

Feel free to fill in the blanks as you work your way through this part, writing your answers right on the pages. Pull out your trusty No. 2 pencil so that you can erase your notes if you make a mistake — or if your memory configuration changes. Or you can always use a ball point pen and buy another copy of this book if you make a mistake!

Step 1: Take Inventory

Follow these steps to take stock of your computer's memory complement:

1. If Windows is running on your computer, exit Windows by choosing File⇨Exit Windows from Program Manager.

2. From the MS-DOS prompt, run the Microsoft Diagnostics program by typing this command:

   msd

   MSD displays the Welcome screen while your computer grunts and grinds.

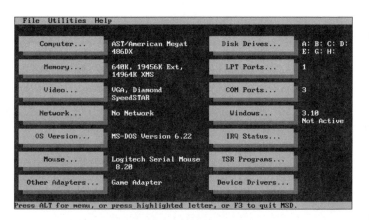

```
 File  Utilities  Help

                    Microsoft (R) Diagnostics
                           Version 2.11
              Copyright (C) Microsoft Corporation, 1990-94
                         All Rights Reserved

         The Microsoft Diagnostics are  designed  to  assist
         Microsoft Product Support  personnel  in  obtaining
         detailed technical information about your computer.

              Thank you for using Microsoft Products.

                  MSD is examining your system ...


MSD is examining your system
```

When the grunting and grinding stops, the Welcome screen
gives way to an informative display. (The screen you see
may vary.)

```
 File  Utilities  Help

   Computer...      AST/American Megat       Disk Drives...     A: B: C: D:
                    486DX                                       E: G: H:

   Memory...        640K, 19456K Ext,        LPT Ports...       1
                    14964K XMS

   Video...         VGA, Diamond             COM Ports...       3
                    SpeedSTAR

   Network...       No Network               Windows...         3.10
                                                                Not Active

   OS Version...    MS-DOS Version 6.22      IRQ Status...

   Mouse...         Logitech Serial Mouse    TSR Programs...
                    8.20

   Other Adapters...  Game Adapter           Device Drivers...

Press ALT for menu, or press highlighted letter, or F3 to quit MSD.
```

3. Take note of your computer's CPU type. This information is
   located just to the right of the big rectangle labelled
   Computer near the top left corner of the display. In the
   preceding example, the CPU type is *486DX*. Mark the CPU
   type on the Memory Report Card that appears at the end of
   this section.

4. Take note of the amount of conventional memory and the amount of extended memory available on your computer. This information is located just to the right of the big rectangle labelled *Memory*. (In the preceding example, the line *640K, 19456K Ext* indicates 640K of conventional memory and 19456K of extended memory.) Record the conventional and extended memory on the Memory Report Card.

5. Use the File⇨Exit command to exit from MSD back to the MS-DOS prompt.

6. From the MS-DOS prompt, type the MEM command:

mem

```
C:\>mem

Memory Type      Total  =  Used  +   Free
----------------  ------    ------     ------
Conventional       640K      177K      463K
Upper              155K       30K      125K
Reserved           384K      384K        0K
Extended (XMS)  19,301K    2,289K   17,012K
----------------  ------    ------     ------
Total memory    20,480K    2,879K   17,601K

Total under 1 MB   795K      206K      589K

Largest executable program size       463K (474,448 bytes)
Largest free upper memory block       125K (128,144 bytes)
MS-DOS is resident in the high memory area.

C:\>
```

7. Take note of the amount of free conventional, upper, and extended (XMS) memory listed in the right-hand column of numbers in the MEM command output. The preceding example shows 463K of free conventional memory, 125K of free upper memory, and 17,012K of free extended memory. Record these numbers on the Memory Report Card that appears at the end of this section. (Oh, if expanded memory is listed, record it, too.)

If you're using MS-DOS 5, the MEM command doesn't display a columnar list of memory statistics as shown in the preceding example. The amount of free conventional memory is stated as the *largest executable program size,* and the amount of available extended memory is listed as *available XMS memory*. The amount of free upper memory is not listed.

8. Decide whether you need expanded memory (EMS). If you use Lotus 1-2-3 Version 2.something or any other really old spreadsheet program, you may need expanded memory. Check your owner's manual to find out. When in doubt, assume that you do *not* need expanded memory. You can always set it up later if you discover you were wrong.

9. Write your answer in the space provided on the Memory Report Card.

Memory Report Card

CPU Type

❏   8088
❏   80286
❏   80386 or 80386SX
❏   i486DX, i486DX2, i486DX4, i486SX or other 486
❏   Pentium or P5
❏   Other: _____

Installed Memory

Base Memory: _____

Extended Memory: _____

Available Memory

Conventional: _____

Upper: _____

Extended (XMS):   _____

Expanded (EMS):   _____

Do You Need Expanded Memory?

_____ Yes, Absotively, Posolutely

_____ No, Not In A Million Years, So Get Off My Back

_____ Gee, I Don't Know; I'll Find Out Later

Step 2: Run MemMaker

MemMaker is the MS-DOS 6 command that makes memory management easy. It is available with all versions of MS-DOS 6 (6.0, 6.2, 6.21, and 6.22). Without MemMaker, you have to twiddle with the CONFIG.SYS and AUTOEXEC.BAT files yourself to configure your memory for optimum use. MemMaker automatically adds whatever commands are necessary in your CONFIG.SYS and AUTOEXEC.BAT files so that whatever memory your computer has is used as efficiently as possible.

Use MemMaker only if your computer has an 80386, i486, or Pentium processor. MemMaker has no effect on computers that use an 8088 or 80286 processor. (Sniff!)

1. Type the following command at the MS-DOS prompt to display the Welcome screen:

   memmaker

```
Microsoft MemMaker

Welcome to MemMaker.

MemMaker optimizes your system's memory by moving memory-resident
programs and device drivers into the upper memory area. This
frees conventional memory for use by applications.

After you run MemMaker, your computer's memory will remain
optimized until you add or remove memory-resident programs or
device drivers. For an optimum memory configuration, run MemMaker
again after making any such changes.

MemMaker displays options as highlighted text. (For example, you
can change the "Continue" option below.) To cycle through the
available options, press SPACEBAR. When MemMaker displays the
option you want, press ENTER.

For help while you are running MemMaker, press F1.

              Continue or Exit? Continue

ENTER=Accept Selection  SPACEBAR=Change Selection  F1=Help  F3=Exit
```

2. Press Enter after you have read the fine print contained within the Welcome screen. MemMaker next asks whether you want to use Express or Custom mode.

```
Microsoft MemMaker

There are two ways to run MemMaker:

Express Setup optimizes your computer's memory automatically.

Custom Setup gives you more control over the changes that
MemMaker makes to your system files. Choose Custom Setup
if you are an experienced user.

            Use Express or Custom Setup? Express Setup




ENTER=Accept Selection  SPACEBAR=Change Selection  F1=Help  F3=Exit
```

3. Press Enter to select Express mode.

Custom mode is for memory management experts who want to fiddle with MemMaker's default settings. See the entry for MemMaker in Part IV for details on using Custom mode.

4. MemMaker next asks whether you want to enable expanded memory (EMS).

```
Microsoft MemMaker

If you use any programs that require expanded memory (EMS), answer
Yes to the following question.  Answering Yes makes expanded memory
available, but might not free as much conventional memory.

If none of your programs need expanded memory, answer No to the
following question.  Answering No makes expanded memory unavailable,
but can free more conventional memory.

If you are not sure whether your programs require expanded memory,
answer No.  If you later discover that a program needs expanded
memory, run MemMaker again and answer Yes to this question.

Do you use any programs that need expanded memory (EMS)? No




ENTER=Accept Selection  SPACEBAR=Change Selection  F1=Help  F3=Exit
```

If you use any old MS-DOS programs that require expanded memory, press the spacebar to change the answer to Yes and then press Enter; otherwise, just press Enter to accept the default answer, which is No.

MemMaker informs you that it is about to restart your computer.

```
Microsoft MemMaker

    MemMaker will now restart your computer.

    If your computer doesn't start properly, just turn it off
    and on again, and MemMaker will recover automatically.
    If a program other than MemMaker starts after your computer
    restarts, exit the program so that MemMaker can continue.

        • Remove any disks from your floppy-disk drives and
          then press ENTER. Your computer will restart.




ENTER=Continue
```

5. Remove any disks in your floppy drives and then press Enter to reboot your computer.

   After your computer reboots, MemMaker comes back to life and shows a count of the different combinations of memory configuration options it is considering.

```
Microsoft MemMaker

    Please wait.  MemMaker is determining the optimum memory
    configuration for your computer and has considered
        253 configuration(s).

    Calculations Complete.
```

MemMaker proudly boasts that it has finished optimizing your memory and asks for your permission to reboot again. Ominous warnings about watching for strange messages appear on-screen after your computer reboots.

Microsoft MemMaker

MemMaker will now restart your computer to test the new memory configuration.

While your computer is restarting, watch your screen carefully. Note any unusual messages or problems. If your computer doesn't start properly, just turn it off and on again, and MemMaker will recover automatically.

  • Remove any disks from your floppy-disk drives and then press ENTER. Your computer will restart.

ENTER=Continue

---

6. Press Enter to restart your computer a second time. After your computer reboots, another peculiar screen is displayed.

7. Does your computer *appear* to be working properly? If so, press Enter. If not, see the troubleshooting tips in Part V.

8. MemMaker finally displays its last screen, which brags about how much MemMaker improved your memory configuration.

```
Microsoft MemMaker

MemMaker has finished optimizing your system's memory. The following
table summarizes the memory use (in bytes) on your system:

                              Before     After
     Memory Type              MemMaker   MemMaker    Change

     Free conventional memory:  474,736    586,784    112,048

     Upper memory:
         Used by programs        30,368    142,160    111,792
         Reserved for Windows         0          0          0
         Reserved for EMS             0          0          0
         Free                   128,192     16,352

     Expanded memory:          Disabled   Disabled

Your original CONFIG.SYS and AUTOEXEC.BAT files have been saved
as CONFIG.UMB and AUTOEXEC.UMB.  If MemMaker changed your Windows
SYSTEM.INI file, the original file was saved as SYSTEM.UMB.

ENTER=Exit  ESC=Undo changes
```

9. Review the statistics shown on the MemMaker brag screen,
   especially the amount of conventional memory available
   before and after running MemMaker. When you're satisfied,
   press Enter. You will at last be returned to the familiar and
   comforting MS-DOS prompt.

   (Or, if you're a Windows-only user, the strange and dis-
   heartening MS-DOS prompt, in which case you can type **win**
   to get back to the happy land of Windows.)

Part II
Common Memory Management Tasks

This part describes the most common memory management tasks. The tasks are grouped into the following categories for easy reference:

Basic tasks	Multiple configurations
Booting	RAM drive
Device drivers	SmartDrive
Expanded memory	Upper memory
Extended memory	Windows memory configuration

The preceding categories are arranged in alphabetical order. Within each category, individual tasks are listed in logical sequence.

Basic Tasks

This section describes some basic memory management tasks, such as finding out how much memory you have, editing your configuration files, and using the MS-DOS 6.0 MemMaker command.

Determining How Much Memory You Have

The following procedures show you how to (1) determine how much memory is actually installed in your computer, and (2) determine how much of that memory is actually available for MS-DOS to use.

The following procedure works only if you have MS-DOS 6.0 or later, or if you have Windows 3.1.

How to do it quickly

At the DOS prompt, type **msd** to display the amount of memory installed on your computer. Type **mem** to display how much memory is available to MS-DOS.

How to do it

To determine how much memory is installed in your computer:

1. If Windows is running on your computer, exit Windows by exiting any active application programs and then using the File⇨Exit Windows command from Program Manager.

2. From the MS-DOS prompt, run the Microsoft Diagnostics program by typing this command:

   msd

   Your computer churns for a few moments while it displays the welcome screen.

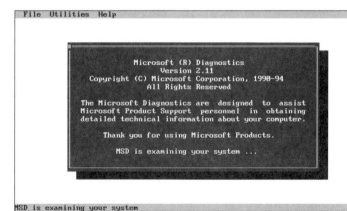

After a few moments, the welcome screen is replaced by an informative display.

```
 File  Utilities  Help

  ┌──────────────────┐  AST/American Megat    ┌──────────────┐  A: B: C: D:
  │    Computer...   │  486DX                 │ Disk Drives...│  E: G: H:
  └──────────────────┘                        └──────────────┘
  ┌──────────────────┐  640K, 19456K Ext,     ┌──────────────┐  1
  │    Memory...     │  14964K XMS            │  LPT Ports...│
  └──────────────────┘                        └──────────────┘
  ┌──────────────────┐  VGA, Diamond          ┌──────────────┐  3
  │     Video...     │  SpeedSTAR            │  COM Ports...│
  └──────────────────┘                        └──────────────┘
  ┌──────────────────┐  No Network            ┌──────────────┐  3.10
  │    Network...    │                       │  Windows...  │  Not Active
  └──────────────────┘                        └──────────────┘
  ┌──────────────────┐  MS-DOS Version 6.22   ┌──────────────┐
  │   OS Version...  │                       │  IRQ Status...│
  └──────────────────┘                        └──────────────┘
  ┌──────────────────┐  Logitech Serial Mouse ┌──────────────┐
  │     Mouse...     │  8.20                 │ TSR Programs...│
  └──────────────────┘                        └──────────────┘
  ┌──────────────────┐  Game Adapter          ┌──────────────┐
  │ Other Adapters...│                       │ Device Drivers...│
  └──────────────────┘                        └──────────────┘

 Press ALT for menu, or press highlighted letter, or F3 to quit MSD.
```

3. Note the amount of conventional memory and the amount of extended memory available on your computer, displayed just to the right of the big rectangle labeled "Memory...." (In the preceding example, the line "640K, 19456K Ext" indicates 640K of conventional memory and 19456K of extended memory.) Record the conventional and extended memory in the following spaces:

   Conventional memory: _____

   Extended memory: _____

4. Choose File⇨Exit to exit from MSD back to the MS-DOS prompt.

To determine how much memory is available for MS-DOS to use:

1. If Windows is running on your computer, exit Windows by exiting any active application programs and then using the File⇨Exit Windows command from Program Manager.

2. Type the MEM command:

   mem

   An informative display appears.

3. Take note of the amount of free conventional, upper, and extended (XMS) memory listed in the rightmost column of numbers in the MEM command output. The above example shows 463K free conventional memory, 125K free upper memory, and 17,012K free extended memory. If expanded memory is available, it is shown, too. Record these numbers in the spaces provided:

```
C:\>mem

Memory Type        Total  =   Used   +   Free
                   -------    -------    -------
Conventional        640K       177K       463K
Upper               155K        30K       125K
Reserved            384K       384K         0K
Extended (XMS)   19,301K     2,289K    17,012K
                   -------    -------    -------
Total memory     20,480K     2,879K    17,601K

Total under 1 MB    795K       206K       589K

Largest executable program size      463K (474,448 bytes)
Largest free upper memory block      125K (128,144 bytes)
MS-DOS is resident in the high memory area.

C:\>
```

Free conventional memory: _____

Free upper memory: _____

Free extended (XMS) memory: _____

If you're using MS-DOS 5, the MEM command doesn't display a
columnar list of memory statistics as shown in the previous
example. Instead, the amount of free conventional memory is
stated as the "largest executable program size" and the amount of
available extended memory is listed as "available XMS memory."
The amount of free upper memory is not listed.

Editing the CONFIG.SYS or AUTOEXEC.BAT File

Many of the configuration procedures described in this book
require that you edit the MS-DOS configuration file CONFIG.SYS or
the start-up batch file AUTOEXEC.BAT. The easiest way to do that
is by using the MS-DOS EDIT command.

The EDIT command is available only under MS-DOS 5.0 and later.

How to do it quickly

At the DOS prompt, type **edit c:\config.sys** or **edit
c:\autoexec.bat,** depending on which file you want to edit.

How to do it

To edit the CONFIG.SYS file, just use the following steps. The procedure for editing AUTOEXEC.BAT is the same, except as noted.

1. If Windows is running on your computer, exit Windows by exiting any active application programs and then choosing File⇨Exit Windows from Program Manager.

2. If the command prompt indicates that the current drive is not drive C, then type the following command and then press Enter to log to drive C:

   c:

3. Type the following command to log to the root directory of drive C:

   **cd **

4. Type the following command to make a backup copy of your CONFIG.SYS file, just in case you make a mistake when editing the file:

   copy config.sys *.old

   If the message "Overwrite CONFIG.OLD (Yes, No, All)?" appears, press Y unless you want to keep the previous backup of the CONFIG.SYS file. In that case, press N and reenter the command substituting a different filename for CONFIG.OLD.

   If you're working with the AUTOEXEC.BAT, type this command instead:

   copy autoexec.bat *.old

5. Type the following command to edit the CONFIG.SYS file:

   edit config.sys

   To edit the AUTOEXEC.BAT, type this command:

   edit autoexec.bat

   The Edit command comes to life, displaying the contents of the file.

6. Now is the time to make your changes to the CONFIG.SYS or AUTOEXEC.BAT file. Exactly what changes need to be made depends on what you're doing, and are suggested by other procedures strewn about in this book. So this step is necessarily vague. The following paragraphs summarize the more common editing techniques:

```
  File  Edit  Search  Options                                          Help
                                    CONFIG.SYS
DEVICE=C:\DOS\HIMEM.SYS /TESTMEM:OFF
DEVICE=C:\DOS\EMM386.EXE NOEMS
BUFFERS=15,0
FILES=8
DOS=UMB
LASTDRIVE=H
FCBS=16,8
DOS=HIGH
STACKS=9,256
SHELL=C:\DOS\COMMAND.COM C:\DOS\ /E:512 /P
DEVICEHIGH=\DEV\MTMCDD.SYS /D:MSCD001 /P:300 /A:0 /M:16 /T:3 /I:5
DEVICEHIGH=D:\WINDOWS\COMMAND\DRVSPACE.SYS /MOVE
DEVICEHIGH=C:\DOS\ANSI.SYS




MS-DOS Editor  <F1=Help> Press ALT to activate menus              N 00001:001
```

To add a new line: Move the cursor to the end of the line you want the new line inserted after (use the up- and down-arrow keys to move the cursor to the correct line; then use the End key to move the cursor to the end of the line). Press Enter to create a new line. Then type whatever command is called for on the line.

To delete a line: Move the cursor to the line you want to delete (it doesn't matter where in the line you place the cursor, so long as the cursor is somewhere in the line you want to delete) and then press Ctrl-Y.

To temporarily disable a line: Move the cursor to the beginning of the line you want to temporarily disable and type the word **REM** followed by a space. The following screen shows a CONFIG.SYS file with the last line temporarily disabled in this way:

To reinstate a disabled line: Move the cursor to the beginning of the line and use the Delete key to delete the word REM.

To move a line: To change the location of a line, position the cursor in the line you want to move, and then press Ctrl-Y to delete the line. Next, move the cursor to the beginning of the line that you want to insert the removed line in front of and press Shift-Insert.

For more information about the EDIT command, consult *DOS For Dummies.*

7. To save your changes, hold down the Alt key and press F, and then press S. This invokes the File⇨Save command.

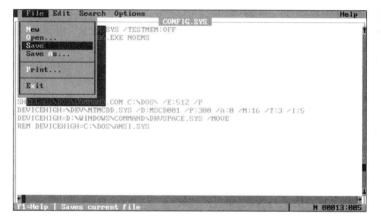

```
File  Edit  Search  Options                                    Help
                          CONFIG.SYS
DEVICE=C:\DOS\HIMEM.SYS /TESTMEM:OFF
DEVICE=C:\DOS\EMM386.EXE NOEMS
BUFFERS=15,0
FILES=8
DOS=UMB
LASTDRIVE=H
FCBS=16,8
DOS=HIGH
STACKS=9,256
SHELL=C:\DOS\COMMAND.COM C:\DOS\ /E:512 /P
DEVICEHIGH=\DEV\MTMCDD.SYS /D:MSCD001 /P:300 /A:0 /M:16 /T:3 /I:5
DEVICEHIGH=D:\WINDOWS\COMMAND\DRVSPACE.SYS /MOVE
REM DEVICEHIGH=C:\DOS\ANSI.SYS




MS-DOS Editor   <F1=Help> Press ALT to activate menus          N 00013:005
```

```
File  Edit  Search  Options                                    Help
                          CONFIG.SYS
New          SYS /TESTMEM:OFF
Open...      6.EXE NOEMS
Save
Save As...

Print...

Exit

SH         DOS\COMMAND   .COM C:\DOS\ /E:512 /P
DEVICEHIGH=\DEV\MTMCDD.SYS /D:MSCD001 /P:300 /A:0 /M:16 /T:3 /I:5
DEVICEHIGH=D:\WINDOWS\COMMAND\DRVSPACE.SYS /MOVE
REM DEVICEHIGH=C:\DOS\ANSI.SYS




F1=Help | Saves current file                                  N 00013:005
```

8. Hold down the Alt key and press F followed by X. This invokes the File⇨Exit command, which allows you to exit the editor and return to the MS-DOS prompt.

9. Press Ctrl-Alt-Delete to reboot your computer so the CONFIG.SYS or AUTOEXEC.BAT changes that you made can take effect.

Booting

This section holds procedures that you can follow to improve your computer's boot process, including such essentials as "clean booting," "quiet booting," and "single-step booting."

Bypassing the ROM-BIOS Memory Check

Whenever you start your computer, the ROM-BIOS performs a memory self-check to make sure that all of the memory installed in your computer is functioning. It's a good idea to allow this check to proceed to completion once in a while, but it's not really necessary to stand idly by while your computer counts up its memory every time you turn it on.

How to do it

Most computers allow you to bypass this memory check and thereby speed up the boot sequence by pressing a key (usually pressing the Escape key or the spacebar does the trick) when you see the memory numbers ticking off. It doesn't work on all computers, so you need to try it to find out if it works on yours.

 This trick is especially useful for impressing your friends. The next time you see your friend twiddling his or her thumbs while waiting for his or her computer to count off its memory — click, click, click — reach over his or her shoulder and quickly press the Escape key. Your friend will be utterly amazed by your computer prowess.

Bypassing the HIMEM.SYS Memory Check

 In MS-DOS 6.22, the HIMEM.SYS device driver, which is responsible for managing extended memory, performs a memory test that is similar to the memory test performed by the ROM-BIOS when you boot your computer. This extra memory test makes doubly sure that your memory is functioning properly, but it adds several annoying seconds to your computer's boot-up time. You can make your computer start up faster by eliminating the HIMEM.SYS memory test.

How to do it quickly

Add /TESTMEM:OFF to the HIMEM.SYS line in your CONFIG.SYS file:

```
device=himem.sys /testmem:off
```

How to do it

1. Exit Windows if Windows is running. This procedure must be performed from an MS-DOS prompt. (Do not double-click on the MS-DOS icon; that starts an MS-DOS session but doesn't actually quit Windows.)

2. Type the following command:

   edit c:\config.sys

3. Find the line that looks something like this:

   ```
   device=c:\dos\himem.sys
   ```

4. Edit that line so that it looks more like this:

   ```
   device=c:\dos\himem.sys /testmem:off
   ```

   The following sample CONFIG.SYS file includes a HIMEM.SYS line that disables the memory test.

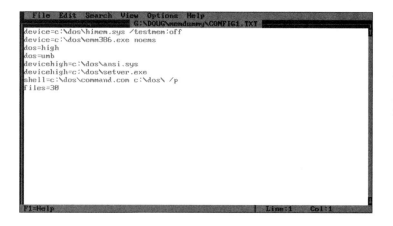

```
 File  Edit  Search  View  Options  Help
                        G:\DOUG\memdummy\CONFIG1.TXT
device=c:\dos\himem.sys /testmem:off
device=c:\dos\emm386.exe noems
dos=high
dos=umb
devicehigh=c:\dos\ansi.sys
devicehigh=c:\dos\setver.exe
shell=c:\dos\command.com c:\dos\ /p
files=30




F1=Help                                              Line:1    Col:1
```

5. Choose File⇨Save to save your modification.

6. Choose File⇨Exit to return to the MS-DOS prompt.

7. Press Ctrl-Alt-Delete to reboot your computer.

8. Say "Whee!" when you notice how much faster your computer boots up.

Bypassing CONFIG.SYS and AUTOEXEC.BAT

If you've accidentally messed up your CONFIG.SYS and AUTOEXEC.BAT file, you can instruct MS-DOS to bypass them at start-up by following this procedure:

How to do it quickly

Press F5 when you see the message `Starting MS-DOS....`

How to do it

1. Exit Windows. Never restart your computer while Windows is running!

2. Press Ctrl-Alt-Delete to reboot your computer.

3. Position your finger over the F5 key.

4. Wait until you see the following message:

   ```
   Starting MS-DOS...
   ```

5. Press and release the F5 key. MS-DOS displays the following reassuring message:

   ```
   MS-DOS is bypassing your CONFIG.SYS and
   AUTOEXEC.BAT files.
   ```

   Eventually, you'll see the normal command prompt.

6. Fix your CONFIG.SYS and/or AUTOEXEC.BAT file so that you can reboot normally.

Processing CONFIG.SYS One Line at a Time

If a particular CONFIG.SYS line seems to be causing difficulties, you can instruct MS-DOS to ask for your permission to process each CONFIG.SYS line. Then, when you get to the line in question, you can tell MS-DOS to skip the line in the hopes that your computer will boot properly.

How to do it quickly

Press F8 when you see the message Starting MS-DOS...

How to do it

The following procedure is useful when troubleshooting memory management problems:

1. Exit Windows. Never restart your computer while Windows is running!

2. Press Ctrl-Alt-Delete to reboot your computer.

3. Position your finger over the F8 key.

4. Wait until you see the following message:

```
Starting MS-DOS...
```

5. Press and release the F8 key. MS-DOS displays the following reassuring message:

```
MS-DOS will prompt you to confirm each
startup command.
```

6. For each command in your CONFIG.SYS file, you are prompted in this fashion:

```
device=c:\dos\himem.sys [Y,N]?
```

   Press Y if you want MS-DOS to process the command; press N if you want the command to be ignored.

   At any time, you can press Esc to process all remaining start-up commands (including AUTOEXEC.BAT) or press F5 to bypass all remaining start-up commands.

   When MS-DOS gets to the end of the CONFIG.SYS file, it asks if you want to process AUTOEXEC.BAT:

```
Process AUTOEXEC.BAT [Y,N]?
```

7. Press Y to process AUTOEXEC.BAT, or press N to skip it.

   For each command in your AUTOEXEC.BAT file, MS-DOS prompts you in this manner:

```
echo off [Y,N]?
```

8. Press Y if you want MS-DOS to process the command; press N if you want the command to be ignored.

Once again, you can press Esc to process all remaining AUTOEXEC.BAT commands, or press F5 to bypass all remaining commands.

Eventually, you see the normal command prompt.

Disabling the Capability to Bypass CONFIG.SYS and AUTOEXEC.BAT

 If you're responsible for supporting someone else's computer, you may not want that someone else to be able to bypass CONFIG.SYS and AUTOEXEC.BAT when they boot. In that case, you can disable that capability using this procedure.

How to do it quickly

Add a SWITCHES command to your CONFIG.SYS file:

```
switches=/n
```

How to do it

If you want to prevent users from using F5 to bypass configuration files or F8 to selectively bypass configuration commands, use this procedure:

1. Exit Windows if Windows is running. This procedure must be performed from an MS-DOS prompt.

2. Type the following command:

   edit c:\config.sys

3. Add the following line to the CONFIG.SYS file:

```
switches=/n
```

It doesn't matter whether you put this command at the top, bottom, or in the middle of CONFIG.SYS. Put it in whatever location makes you happy.

The following sample CONFIG.SYS file includes a SWITCHES line to disable F5 and F8.

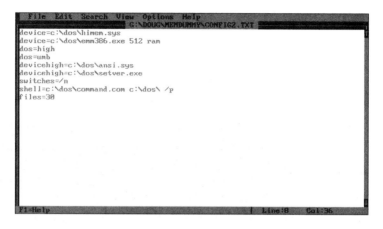

```
 File  Edit  Search  View  Options  Help
                    G:\DOUG\MEMDUMMY\CONFIG2.TXT
device=c:\dos\himem.sys
device=c:\dos\emm386.exe 512 ram
dos=high
dos=umb
devicehigh=c:\dos\ansi.sys
devicehigh=c:\dos\setver.exe
switches=/n
shell=c:\dos\command.com c:\dos\ /p
files=30




F1=Help                                    Line:8   Col:36
```

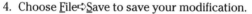

4. Choose File⇨Save to save your modification.

5. Choose File⇨Exit to return to the MS-DOS prompt.

6. Press Ctrl-Alt-Delete to reboot your computer.

7. Go ahead and try to press F5 or F8. Nothing happens!

To enable F5 or F8 once again, remove the SWITCHES=/N line from CONFIG.SYS.

Creating a Panic Disk

Always keep a panic disk — one you can boot your computer from in case something goes awry with your hard disk — nearby.

How to do it quickly

Insert a blank disk in drive A and type the command **format a: /s**. Then copy the following files to the disk:

```
autoexec.bat

config.sys

fdisk.exe a:

format.com a:
```

(continued)

```
attrib.exe a:

chkdsk.exe a:        (MS-DOS 6.0 and earlier)

scandisk.* a:        (MS-DOS 6.2 and later)
```

How to do it

1. Format a diskette in drive A by using the following command:

   format a: /s

2. Copy your CONFIG.SYS file to the A drive by using this command:

   copy config.sys a:

3. Copy your AUTOEXEC.BAT file to the A drive by using this command:

   copy autoexec.bat a:

4. Use the following commands to copy vital MS-DOS trouble-shooting commands to the diskette:

   copy \dos\fdisk.exe a:

   copy \dos\format.com a:

   copy \dos\attrib.exe a:

   copy \dos\chkdsk.exe a: (MS-DOS 6.0 and earlier)

   copy \dos\scandisk.* a: (MS-DOS 6.2 and later)

5. Leave the panic disk in drive A and press Ctrl-Alt-Delete to reboot your computer. It should boot up properly from the panic disk.

6. Remove the panic disk from drive A and press Ctrl-Alt-Delete to reboot your computer again.

Make sure that you have a copy of your backup program available on diskette. If you lose the data on your hard drive (heaven forbid!), you'll need a diskette copy of your backup program to restore data from a recent backup.

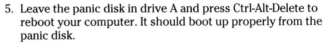

Device Drivers

This section contains procedures for adding and removing MS-DOS device drivers.

Adding a Device Driver

The following procedure explains how to add a device driver to your memory configuration.

How to do it quickly

Add a **devicehigh=** line that names the driver you want loaded to your CONFIG.SYS file. For example,

```
devicehigh=c:\dos\ansi.sys
```

How to do it

1. Exit Windows if Windows is running. This procedure must be performed from an MS-DOS prompt.

2. Type the following command:

   edit c:\config.sys

3. Use the following table to determine which line to add to CONFIG.SYS to activate the driver that you need:

MS-DOS Device Drivers

Driver	Required CONFIG.SYS Line
ANSI.SYS	devicehigh=c:\dos\ansi.sys
CHKSTATE.SYS	devicehigh=c:\dos\chkstate.sys
DBLSPACE.SYS	devicehigh=c:\dos\dblspace.sys
DRVSPACE.SYS	devicehigh=c:\dos\drvspace.sys
DRIVER.SYS	devicehigh=c:\dos\driver.sys
EGA.SYS	devicehigh=c:\dos\ega.sys
EMM386.EXE	device=c:\dos\emm386.exe
HIMEM.SYS	device=c:\dos\himem.sys
INTERLNK.EXE	devicehigh=c:\dos\interlnk.exe
POWER.EXE	devicehigh=c:\dos\power.exe
RAMDRIVE.SYS	devicehigh=c:\dos\ramdrive.sys
SETVER.EXE	devicehigh=c:\dos\setver.exe
SMARTDRV.EXE	device=c:\dos\smartdrv.exe /double_buffer

4. Determine the location at which you want to add the line that you selected in step 3. Most device drivers can be inserted into CONFIG.SYS at any location. If your CONFIG.SYS file includes HIMEM.SYS, however, the HIMEM.SYS line should appear before any other DEVICE or DEVICEHIGH lines.

5. Insert the line you selected in step 3 at the location you selected in step 4. The following sample CONFIG.SYS file includes DEVICEHIGH commands to load the ANSI.SYS and SETVER drivers.

6. Choose File⇨Save to save your changes.

7. Choose File⇨Exit to return to the MS-DOS prompt.

8. Press Ctrl-Alt-Delete to reboot your computer.

9. To verify that the device driver was loaded properly, type the following command at the command prompt:

   mem /c /p

   A memory listing such as the following is displayed.

10. Locate the newly installed driver in the list of active device drivers displayed by the MEM /C/P command.

```
Modules using memory below 1 MB:

Name            Total    =  Conventional  +  Upper Memory
-------------  --------    ------------     -------------
MSDOS          15,725  (15K)   15,725  (15K)        0   (0K)
HIMEM           1,168   (1K)    1,168   (1K)        0   (0K)
EMM386          3,120   (3K)    3,120   (3K)        0   (0K)
COMMAND         3,184   (3K)    3,184   (3K)        0   (0K)
MSCDEX         28,288  (28K)   28,288  (28K)        0   (0K)
MOUSE          17,088  (17K)   17,088  (17K)        0   (0K)
MTMCDD         50,800  (50K)        0   (0K)   50,800  (50K)
DRVSPACE       39,888  (39K)        0   (0K)   39,888  (39K)
SMARTDRV       30,368  (30K)        0   (0K)   30,368  (30K)
SHARE          16,944  (17K)        0   (0K)   16,944  (17K)
Free          607,184 (593K)  586,592 (573K)   20,592  (20K)

Memory Summary:

Type of Memory    Total    =    Used    +    Free
--------------   --------      --------     --------
Conventional      655,360       68,768      586,592
Upper             158,592      138,000       20,592
Reserved          393,216      393,216            0
Press any key to continue . . .
```

Removing a Device Driver

How to do it quickly

Remove the **device=** or **devicehigh=** line that names the driver
you want loaded from your CONFIG.SYS file, or add the word REM
to it:

```
rem devicehigh=c:\dos\ansi.sys
```

How to do it

1. Exit Windows if Windows is running. This procedure must
   be performed from an MS-DOS prompt.

2. Type the following command:

   edit c:\config.sys

3. Move the cursor to the beginning of the line that you want
   to delete.

4. To permanently remove the device driver, press Ctrl-Y.

   To temporarily remove the device driver, add the word
   REM to the beginning of the line. For example,

```
rem devicehigh=c:\dos\ansi.sys
```

The following sample CONFIG.SYS file shows DEVICEHIGH commands to load the ANSI.SYS and SETVER drivers temporarily disabled.

```
 File  Edit  Search  View  Options  Help
                  G:\DOUG\MEMDUMMY\CONFIG4.TXT
device=c:\dos\himem.sys
device=c:\dos\emm386.exe noems
dos=high
dos=umb
rem devicehigh=c:\dos\ansi.sys
rem devicehigh=c:\dos\setver.exe
shell=c:\dos\command.com c:\dos\ /p
files=30




F1=Help                                    | Line:8    Col:1
```

5. Choose File⇨Save to save your changes.

6. Choose File⇨Exit to return to the MS-DOS prompt.

7. Press Ctrl-Alt-Delete to reboot your computer.

Extended Memory

The procedures in this section show you how to activate and use extended memory using HIMEM.SYS, the extended memory provider that comes with Windows 3.1 as well as MS-DOS 5 and 6.

Activating Extended Memory (XMS)

Although your computer may have megabytes of extended memory, MS-DOS and programs that run under MS-DOS are not able to utilize that memory unless you activate a special program called an *extended memory provider*. Fortunately, Windows 3.1 as well as both MS-DOS 5 and 6 come with just such a program, named HIMEM.SYS.

Extended Memory

Any memory beyond the first 1MB of memory on an 80286 or later computer. If you buy a computer with 4MB of memory, you get 3MB of extended memory. My computer with 20MB of memory has 19MB of extended memory.

How to do it quickly

Add the following line to your CONFIG.SYS file:

```
device=c:\dos\himem.sys
```

How to do it

1. Exit Windows if Windows is running.

2. Type the following command:

   edit c:\config.sys

3. If you are using MS-DOS 6.*x,* add the following line at the top of the CONFIG.SYS file:

   device=c:\dos\himem.sys

   Use the preceding line if you have MS-DOS 5 and do *not* have Windows 3.1. If you use a version of MS-DOS earlier than 6.0 but you also use Windows 3.1, add this line instead:

```
device=c:\windows\himem.sys
```

The trick is to use the newest available HIMEM.SYS version, whether it resides in your \WINDOWS or \DOS directory.

4. While you're at it, you may as well add this line:

```
dos=high
```

This line places portions of MS-DOS in the High Memory Area, thus increasing the amount of free conventional memory. It can appear anywhere after the line inserted in step 3.

For more information about DOS=HIGH, see the procedure, "Loading DOS into the High Memory Area (HMA)," which appears next.

The following sample CONFIG.SYS file includes HIMEM and DOS=HIGH lines to activate XMS memory and load DOS into the HMA.

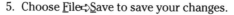

```
 File  Edit  Search  View  Options  Help
                    G:\DOUG\MEMDUMMY\CONFIG5.TXT
device=c:\dos\himem.sys
device=c:\dos\emm386.exe noems
dos=high
dos=umb
devicehigh=c:\dos\ansi.sys
devicehigh=c:\dos\setver.exe
shell=c:\dos\command.com c:\dos\ /p
files=30




 F1=Help                                        Line:7    Col:36
```

5. Choose File⇨Save to save your changes.

6. Choose File⇨Exit to return to the MS-DOS prompt.

7. Press Ctrl-Alt-Delete to reboot your computer.

8. Run the MEM command to verify that XMS memory is available.

Loading DOS into the High Memory Area (HMA)

If your computer has extended memory, you can free up some conventional memory by relocating a portion of MS-DOS into a special area of extended memory called the *High Memory Area*.

High Memory

The first 64K of extended memory can be used almost as if it were extra conventional memory by utilizing an advanced programming technique formally known as "smoke and mirrors." Smoke and mirrors works only on 386 or better computers. The 64K in question is often referred to as the *high memory area*, or *HMA*.

How to do it quickly

Add the following line to your CONFIG.SYS file:

```
dos=high
```

You must also include a **device=c:\dos\himem.sys** line.

How to do it

1. Exit Windows, if Windows is running, by choosing File⇨Exit.

2. Type the following command:

   edit c:\config.sys

3. Add the following line to your CONFIG.SYS file:

```
dos=high
```

   This line can be inserted anywhere in your CONFIG.SYS
   file, but it is usually placed following the
   DEVICE=C:\DOS\HIMEM.SYS command.

   Note that the commands DOS=HIGH and DOS=UMB can be
   combined as DOS=HIGH,UMB (or, if you want to be impetu-
   ous, DOS=UMB,HIGH).

   The following sample CONFIG.SYS file includes HIMEM and
   DOS=HIGH lines to activate XMS memory and load DOS into
   the HMA.

```
                                    CONFIG.SYS
device=c:\dos\himem.sys
device=c:\dos\emm386.exe noems
dos=high
dos=umb
devicehigh=c:\dos\ansi.sys
devicehigh=c:\dos\setver.exe
shell=c:\dos\command.com c:\dos\ p:
files=30




MS-DOS Editor  <F1=Help> Press ALT to activate menus
```

4. Choose File➪Save to save your changes.

5. Choose File➪Exit to return to the MS-DOS prompt.

6. Press Ctrl-Alt-Delete to reboot your computer.

7. Run the MEM command to see how much conventional memory you've freed up.

Expanded Memory

The procedures in this section show you how to use your computer's extended memory to simulate old-style expanded memory that is required by some outdated programs such as Lotus 1-2-3 Version 2.x, as well as some newer game programs.

You must have a 386 or better computer to simulate expanded memory by using extended memory. Although 80286 computers are sophisticated enough to support extended memory, they don't have the ability to use it to simulate expanded memory.

If your computer is equipped with an expanded memory card, you need to consult the documentation that came with the card to configure it properly. However, simulated expanded memory is actually much faster than real expanded memory. So if your computer has sufficient extended memory, you should consider throwing that old expanded memory card into the dumpster and using simulated expanded memory instead. (Better yet, upgrade your old software to a newer version that can utilize extended memory directly.)

Expanded Memory

A special type of memory that was used long ago to provide additional memory for 8088-type computers. True expanded memory resides on a special card that is inserted into one of the computer's expansion slots. However, 386 or better computers can use extended memory to simulate expanded memory. Expanded memory is also known as EMS memory, which stands for Expanded Memory Specification.

Simulating Expanded Memory

You can use extended memory to simulate expanded memory by using this procedure.

How to do it quickly

Add the following lines to your CONFIG.SYS file:

```
device=c:\dos\himem.sys
device=c:\dos\emm386.exe
```

How to do it

The following procedure shows how to use extended memory to simulate expanded memory:

1. Exit Windows if Windows is running (File⇨Exit). This procedure must be performed from an MS-DOS prompt.

2. Type the following command:

   edit c:\config.sys

3. Make sure that one of the following two lines is present in the CONFIG.SYS file:

   ```
   device=c:\dos\himem.sys
   device=c:\windows\himem.sys
   ```

If you cannot find this line, refer to the procedure "Activating Extended Memory" earlier in this part. There, you can find instructions for inserting the line, plus a discussion of which version of HIMEM.SYS to use if two versions of it are present on your computer.

4. Insert the following line in the CONFIG.SYS file, at any location following the HIMEM.SYS line located in step 3:

   ```
   device=c:\dos\emm386.exe
   ```

If you want to activate upper memory as well as expanded memory, use the following line instead:

```
device=c:\dos\emm386.exe ram
```

You can also specify an amount of expanded memory to simulate. For example,

```
device=c:\dos\emm386.exe 512 ram
```

Here, 512K of expanded memory is simulated. If you omit the amount, EMM386.EXE creates as much simulated expanded memory as possible.

If you use MS-DOS Version 5.0 or earlier and you have Windows 3.1, specify `c:\windows\emm386.exe` instead of `c:\dos\emm386.exe` in the preceding examples.

The following sample CONFIG.SYS file includes an EMM386.EXE line that simulates 512K expanded memory and activates upper memory.

```
  File  Edit  Search  View  Options  Help
                      G:\DOUG\MEMDUMMY\CONFIG6.TXT
device=c:\dos\himem.sys
device=c:\dos\emm386.exe noems
dos=high
dos=umb
devicehigh=c:\dos\ansi.sys
devicehigh=c:\dos\setver.exe
shell=c:\dos\command.com c:\dos\ /p
files=30



F1=Help                                        Line:7    Col:36
```

5. Choose File⇨Save to save your changes.

6. Choose File⇨Exit to return to the MS-DOS prompt.

7. Press Ctrl-Alt-Delete to reboot your computer.

8. Run the MEM command to verify that expanded memory is now available.

More stuff

 The EMM386.EXE CONFIG.SYS line is also used to activate the upper memory block; see the procedure "Activating Upper Memory" later in this part for more information.

 EMM386.EXE can be tricky to configure properly on some computers. If your computer doesn't seem to function properly after installing EMM386.EXE, consult the troubleshooting procedures in Part V.

Temporarily Disabling Simulated Expanded Memory

You can temporarily disable expanded memory support from the command line by using this procedure.

How to do it quickly

Type the following command at the DOS prompt:

emm386 off

How to do it

1. Exit Windows if Windows is running (File⇨Exit). This procedure should be carried out from an MS-DOS prompt with Windows not running.

2. Type the following command:

    emm386 off

3. Do whatever it is you want to do with expanded memory disabled (for example, run a program that can access extended memory directly).

4. To restore expanded memory support, type this command:

    emm386 on

More stuff

 The EMM386.EXE program must be included in your CONFIG.SYS file for the EMM386 command to work properly. Refer to "Simulating Expanded Memory" for more information.

MemMaker

 MemMaker is the new MS-DOS 6 command that takes care of optimizing your memory configuration automatically. I spare you the details of making sure your CONFIG.SYS file contains the correct HIMEM.SYS and EMM386.EXE options and DEVICEHIGH commands to cram as many programs and device drivers into upper memory as possible. The procedures in this section cover the use of MemMaker in Express and Custom modes, as well as the procedure for using it when your CONFIG.SYS file includes configuration menus. In addition, you'll find the procedure for undoing MemMaker's changes in case you don't like the results of MemMaker's changes.

Note that MemMaker works only on computers that have a 386 or better processor.

Before you run MemMaker, you should review all of the device drivers that are loaded in your CONFIG.SYS file. You may discover drivers that you don't need. If so, remove them by following the procedure "Removing a Device Driver," which appears in the section "Device Drivers" earlier in this part. You should also remove any unnecessary memory-resident programs that are loaded in your AUTOEXEC.BAT file.

Optimizing Memory with MemMaker

 If your computer has an 80386, i486, or Pentium processor, you can use the MemMaker command to optimize your memory configuration automatically.

How to do it quickly

Type **memmaker** at the DOS prompt and then follow the instructions on-screen.

How to do it

1. Type the following command at the MS-DOS prompt:

   memmaker

   The welcome screen appears.

2. After you have read the fine print contained within the welcome screen, press Enter. MemMaker asks whether you want to use Express or Custom mode.

```
Microsoft MemMaker

Welcome to MemMaker.

MemMaker optimizes your system's memory by moving memory-resident
programs and device drivers into the upper memory area. This
frees conventional memory for use by applications.

After you run MemMaker, your computer's memory will remain
optimized until you add or remove memory-resident programs or
device drivers. For an optimum memory configuration, run MemMaker
again after making any such changes.

MemMaker displays options as highlighted text. (For example, you
can change the "Continue" option below.) To cycle through the
available options, press SPACEBAR. When MemMaker displays the
option you want, press ENTER.

For help while you are running MemMaker, press F1.

            Continue or Exit? Continue

ENTER=Accept Selection  SPACEBAR=Change Selection  F1=Help  F3=Exit
```

```
Microsoft MemMaker

There are two ways to run MemMaker:

Express Setup optimizes your computer's memory automatically.

Custom Setup gives you more control over the changes that
MemMaker makes to your system files. Choose Custom Setup
if you are an experienced user.

            Use Express or Custom Setup? Express Setup

ENTER=Accept Selection  SPACEBAR=Change Selection  F1=Help  F3=Exit
```

3. Press Enter to select Express mode. MemMaker asks whether you want to enable expanded memory (EMS).

Custom mode is for memory management experts who want to fiddle with MemMaker's default settings. See the entry for MemMaker in Part IV for details on using Custom mode.

4. If you use any older MS-DOS programs that require expanded memory, press the spacebar to change the answer to Yes and then press Enter. Otherwise, just press Enter to accept the default answer (No). MemMaker informs you that it is about to restart your computer:

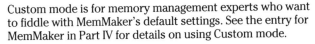

```
Microsoft MemMaker

    If you use any programs that require expanded memory (EMS), answer
    Yes to the following question.  Answering Yes makes expanded memory
    available, but might not free as much conventional memory.

    If none of your programs need expanded memory, answer No to the
    following question.  Answering No makes expanded memory unavailable,
    but can free more conventional memory.

    If you are not sure whether your programs require expanded memory,
    answer No.  If you later discover that a program needs expanded
    memory, run MemMaker again and answer Yes to this question.

    Do you use any programs that need expanded memory (EMS)? No


ENTER=Accept Selection  SPACEBAR=Change Selection  F1=Help  F3=Exit
```

```
Microsoft MemMaker

    MemMaker will now restart your computer.

    If your computer doesn't start properly, just turn it off
    and on again, and MemMaker will recover automatically.
    If a program other than MemMaker starts after your computer
    restarts, exit the program so that MemMaker can continue.

      • Remove any disks from your floppy-disk drives and
        then press ENTER. Your computer will restart.


ENTER=Continue
```

5. Remove any disks from your floppy drives and then press Enter to reboot your computer.

6. After your computer reboots, MemMaker comes back to life and shows a count of the different combinations of memory configuration options it is considering.

```
Microsoft MemMaker

Please wait.  MemMaker is determining the optimum memory
configuration for your computer and has considered
      253 configuration(s).

Calculations Complete.
```

When it is finished, MemMaker proudly boasts that it has finished optimizing your memory. It then asks for your permission to reboot again.

7. Press Enter to restart your computer again. Note the ominous warnings about watching for strange messages when your computer reboots.

```
Microsoft MemMaker

MemMaker will now restart your computer to test the new memory
configuration.

While your computer is restarting, watch your screen carefully.
Note any unusual messages or problems. If your computer doesn't
start properly, just turn it off and on again, and MemMaker
will recover automatically.

  • Remove any disks from your floppy-disk drives and
    then press ENTER. Your computer will restart.

ENTER=Continue
```

After your computer reboots, another peculiar screen is displayed.

8. Does your computer *appear* to be working properly? If so, press Enter.

MemMaker finally displays its last screen, in which it brags about how much it improved your memory configuration.

```
Microsoft MemMaker


    Your computer has just restarted with its new memory configuration.
    Some or all of your device drivers and memory-resident programs
    are now running in upper memory.

    If your system appears to be working properly, choose "Yes."
    If you noticed any unusual messages when your computer started,
    or if your system is not working properly, choose "No."

    Does your system appear to be working properly? Yes




ENTER=Accept Selection  SPACEBAR=Change Selection  F1=Help  F3=Exit
```

```
Microsoft MemMaker


    MemMaker has finished optimizing your system's memory. The following
    table summarizes the memory use (in bytes) on your system:

                                   Before      After
    Memory Type                    MemMaker    MemMaker    Change

    Free conventional memory:      474,736     586,784     112,048

    Upper memory:
      Used by programs              30,368     142,160     111,792
      Reserved for Windows               0           0           0
      Reserved for EMS                   0           0           0
      Free                         128,192      16,352

    Expanded memory:              Disabled    Disabled

    Your original CONFIG.SYS and AUTOEXEC.BAT files have been saved
    as CONFIG.UMB and AUTOEXEC.UMB.  If MemMaker changed your Windows
    SYSTEM.INI file, the original file was saved as SYSTEM.UMB.

ENTER=Exit  ESC=Undo changes
```

9. Review the statistics shown on the MemMaker brag screen, especially the amount of conventional memory available before and after running MemMaker. When you're satisfied, press Enter. You are at last returned to the MS-DOS prompt.

Optimizing Memory with MemMaker's Express Setup Mode

You can optimize memory with MemMaker's Express Setup Mode by following this procedure.

How to do it quickly

Type **memmaker** at the DOS prompt; then follow the instructions on the screen.

How to do it

The easiest way to optimize your memory is to use MemMaker's express setup mode. Just follow these steps:

1. Type the following command at the MS-DOS prompt:

    memmaker

    The welcome screen is displayed.

```
Microsoft MemMaker

Welcome to MemMaker.

MemMaker optimizes your system's memory by moving memory-resident
programs and device drivers into the upper memory area. This
frees conventional memory for use by applications.

After you run MemMaker, your computer's memory will remain
optimized until you add or remove memory-resident programs or
device drivers. For an optimum memory configuration, run MemMaker
again after making any such changes.

MemMaker displays options as highlighted text. (For example, you
can change the "Continue" option below.) To cycle through the
available options, press SPACEBAR. When MemMaker displays the
option you want, press ENTER.

For help while you are running MemMaker, press F1.

              Continue or Exit? Continue

ENTER=Accept Selection  SPACEBAR=Change Selection  F1=Help  F3=Exit
```

2. Press Enter when you have read the fine print contained within the welcome screen. MemMaker next asks if you want to use Express or Custom mode.

3. Press Enter to select Express mode.

    Custom mode is useful if you want to fiddle with MemMaker's default settings. See the procedure "Optimizing Memory with MemMaker's Custom Setup Mode" later in this section for details on using custom mode.

    MemMaker next asks whether you want to enable expanded memory (EMS).

4. If you use any older MS-DOS programs that require expanded memory, press the spacebar to change the answer to Yes; then press Enter. Otherwise, just press Enter to accept the default answer (No).

```
Microsoft MemMaker

   There are two ways to run MemMaker:

   Express Setup optimizes your computer's memory automatically.

   Custom Setup gives you more control over the changes that
   MemMaker makes to your system files. Choose Custom Setup
   if you are an experienced user.

              Use Express or Custom Setup? Express Setup




ENTER=Accept Selection  SPACEBAR=Change Selection  F1=Help  F3=Exit
```

```
Microsoft MemMaker

   If you use any programs that require expanded memory (EMS), answer
   Yes to the following question.  Answering Yes makes expanded memory
   available, but might not free as much conventional memory.

   If none of your programs need expanded memory, answer No to the
   following question.  Answering No makes expanded memory unavailable,
   but can free more conventional memory.

   If you are not sure whether your programs require expanded memory,
   answer No.  If you later discover that a program needs expanded
   memory, run MemMaker again and answer Yes to this question.

   Do you use any programs that need expanded memory (EMS)? No



ENTER=Accept Selection  SPACEBAR=Change Selection  F1=Help  F3=Exit
```

MemMaker next informs you that it is about to restart your computer.

5. Remove any disks in your floppy drives; then press Enter to reboot your computer.

   After your computer reboots, MemMaker will come back to life and show a count of the different combinations of memory configuration options it is considering.

   When it is finished, MemMaker will proudly boast that it has finished optimizing your memory and then ask for your permission to reboot again. Note the ominous warnings about watching for strange messages when your computer reboots.

Microsoft MemMaker

MemMaker will now restart your computer.

If your computer doesn't start properly, just turn it off
and on again, and MemMaker will recover automatically.
If a program other than MemMaker starts after your computer
restarts, exit the program so that MemMaker can continue.

- Remove any disks from your floppy-disk drives and
  then press ENTER. Your computer will restart.

ENTER=Continue

Microsoft MemMaker

Please wait. MemMaker is determining the optimum memory
configuration for your computer and has considered
      253 configuration(s).

Calculations Complete.

Microsoft MemMaker

MemMaker will now restart your computer to test the new memory
configuration.

While your computer is restarting, watch your screen carefully.
Note any unusual messages or problems. If your computer doesn't
start properly, just turn it off and on again, and MemMaker
will recover automatically.

- Remove any disks from your floppy-disk drives and
  then press ENTER. Your computer will restart.

ENTER=Continue

Press the Enter key to restart your computer a second time.

8. After your computer reboots, another peculiar screen is displayed.

```
Microsoft MemMaker
_____

Your computer has just restarted with its new memory configuration.
Some or all of your device drivers and memory-resident programs
are now running in upper memory.

If your system appears to be working properly, choose "Yes."
If you noticed any unusual messages when your computer started,
or if your system is not working properly, choose "No."

Does your system appear to be working properly? Yes



ENTER=Accept Selection  SPACEBAR=Change Selection  F1=Help  F3=Exit
```

9. Does your computer *appear* to be working properly? If so, press the Enter key.

10. MemMaker finally displays its last screen, in which it brags about how much it improved your memory configuration.

```
Microsoft MemMaker
_____

MemMaker has finished optimizing your system's memory. The following
table summarizes the memory use (in bytes) on your system:

                          Before     After
Memory Type              MemMaker   MemMaker    Change
                         _____   _____    _____
Free conventional memory: 474,736   586,784    112,048

Upper memory:
   Used by programs        30,368   142,160    111,792
   Reserved for Windows         0         0          0
   Reserved for EMS             0         0          0
   Free                   128,192    16,352

Expanded memory:         Disabled   Disabled

Your original CONFIG.SYS and AUTOEXEC.BAT files have been saved
as CONFIG.UMB and AUTOEXEC.UMB.  If MemMaker changed your Windows
SYSTEM.INI file, the original file was saved as SYSTEM.UMB.

ENTER=Exit  ESC=Undo changes
```

11. Review the statistics shown on the MemMaker brag screen, especially the amount of conventional memory available before and after running MemMaker. When you're satisfied, press Enter. You will at last be returned to the familiar MS-DOS prompt.

Optimizing Memory With MemMaker's Custom Setup Mode

MemMaker's Custom Setup mode lets you control advanced options. Use Custom Setup mode if you meet any of the following conditions:

• You have an EGA or a VGA monitor (but not a super VGA).

• You do not run MS-DOS programs from within Windows.

• You have previously added an I or X parameter to EMM386.EXE and you want to leave the inclusion or exclusion in effect.

• You have encountered a problem running MemMaker and you want to use less aggressive options.

How to do it quickly

Type **memmaker** at the DOS prompt; then follow the instructions on the screen. When asked whether to use Custom Setup or Express Setup, choose Custom Setup. Then select the advanced options you wish to use.

How to do it

1. Type the following command at the MS-DOS prompt:

    memmaker

    The welcome screen will be displayed.

2. Press Enter. MemMaker next asks if you want to use Express or Custom mode.

3. Press the spacebar to select Custom mode and then press Enter. MemMaker next asks whether you want to enable expanded memory (EMS).

```
Microsoft MemMaker

Welcome to MemMaker.

MemMaker optimizes your system's memory by moving memory-resident
programs and device drivers into the upper memory area. This
frees conventional memory for use by applications.

After you run MemMaker, your computer's memory will remain
optimized until you add or remove memory-resident programs or
device drivers. For an optimum memory configuration, run MemMaker
again after making any such changes.

MemMaker displays options as highlighted text. (For example, you
can change the "Continue" option below.) To cycle through the
available options, press SPACEBAR. When MemMaker displays the
option you want, press ENTER.

For help while you are running MemMaker, press F1.

               Continue or Exit? Continue

ENTER=Accept Selection  SPACEBAR=Change Selection  F1=Help  F3=Exit
```

```
Microsoft MemMaker

There are two ways to run MemMaker:

Express Setup optimizes your computer's memory automatically.

Custom Setup gives you more control over the changes that
MemMaker makes to your system files. Choose Custom Setup
if you are an experienced user.

          Use Express or Custom Setup? Custom Setup




ENTER=Accept Selection  SPACEBAR=Change Selection  F1=Help  F3=Exit
```

```
Microsoft MemMaker

If you use any programs that require expanded memory (EMS), answer
Yes to the following question. Answering Yes makes expanded memory
available, but might not free as much conventional memory.

If none of your programs need expanded memory, answer No to the
following question. Answering No makes expanded memory unavailable,
but can free more conventional memory.

If you are not sure whether your programs require expanded memory,
answer No. If you later discover that a program needs expanded
memory, run MemMaker again and answer Yes to this question.

Do you use any programs that need expanded memory (EMS)? No




ENTER=Accept Selection  SPACEBAR=Change Selection  F1=Help  F3=Exit
```

4. If you use any older MS-DOS programs that require expanded memory, press the spacebar to change the answer to Yes and then press Enter; otherwise, just press Enter to accept the default answer (No).

5. MemMaker next displays a menu of Advanced Options.

```
Microsoft MemMaker

                       Advanced Options

Specify which drivers and TSRs to include in optimization?    No
Scan the upper memory area aggressively?                      Yes
Optimize upper memory for use with Windows?                   Yes
Use monochrome region (B000-B7FF) for running programs?       Yes
Keep current EMM386 memory exclusions and inclusions?         Yes
Move Extended BIOS Data Area from conventional to upper memory? Yes


To select a different option, press the UP ARROW or DOWN ARROW key.
To accept all the settings and continue, press ENTER.



ENTER=Accept All  SPACEBAR=Change Selection  F1=Help  F3=Exit
```

The following paragraphs describe what each of these options does:

Specify which drivers and TSRs to include in optimization? Change this setting to Yes if you are having trouble with a particular device driver or memory-resident program. Then, when MemMaker prompts you for each device driver or program, tell it to exclude the one that's causing you grief.

Scan the upper memory area aggressively? If your system locks up when you restart it or when MemMaker reboots, set this option to No. This tells MemMaker to avoid those portions of upper memory which are most likely to cause memory conflicts.

Optimize upper memory for use with Windows? Change this setting to Yes if you run MS-DOS programs from within Windows. This may result in less memory available for application programs that run outside of Windows but will provide more conventional memory for DOS programs running from within Windows.

Use monochrome region (B000-B7FF) for running programs? Change this setting to Yes if you have an EGA or VGA monitor (but not a super VGA monitor).

Keep current EMM386 memory exclusions and inclusions? Change this option to Yes if you've specified upper memory exclusions or inclusions via the X or I parameters for EMM386 and you want MemMaker to honor your exclusions and/or inclusions.

Move Extended BIOS Data Area from conventional to upper memory? This option moves a 1K memory area called the Extended BIOS Data Area into upper memory. If your computer won't run after MemMaker finishes, change this setting to No.

6. Use the up- and down- arrow keys to move the highlight to an option you want to change; then use the spacebar to change the option's setting. When you're ready, press Enter to continue.

7. If Windows is installed on your computer, MemMaker displays the directory that contains Windows:

```
Microsoft MemMaker


  MemMaker found a copy of Windows in the following directory:

    C:\WINDOWS

    • If this is the copy of Windows you are currently using,
      press ENTER to continue.

    • If your current copy of Windows is in a different directory,
      type the path of that directory, and then press ENTER.








ENTER=Continue  F1=Help  F3=Exit
```

If this is the correct name of the directory that contains Windows, press Enter. Otherwise, type the correct directory information and press Enter.

8. MemMaker next informs you that it is about to restart your computer.

```
Microsoft MemMaker

  MemMaker will now restart your computer.

  If your computer doesn't start properly, just turn it off
  and on again, and MemMaker will recover automatically.
  If a program other than MemMaker starts after your computer
  restarts, exit the program so that MemMaker can continue.

     • Remove any disks from your floppy-disk drives and
       then press ENTER. Your computer will restart.



ENTER=Continue
```

Remove any disks in your floppy drives; then press Enter to reboot your computer.

9. After your computer reboots, MemMaker will come back to life and show a count of the different combinations of memory configuration options it is considering.

```
Microsoft MemMaker

  MemMaker found a copy of Windows in the following directory:

    C:\WINDOWS

     • If this is the copy of Windows you are currently using,
       press ENTER to continue.

     • If your current copy of Windows is in a different directory,
       type the path of that directory, and then press ENTER.




ENTER=Continue  F1=Help  F3=Exit
```

When it is finished, MemMaker will proudly boast that it has finished optimizing your memory and then ask for your permission to reboot again. Note the ominous warnings about watching for strange messages when your computer reboots.

```
Microsoft MemMaker


 MemMaker will now restart your computer.

 If your computer doesn't start properly, just turn it off
 and on again, and MemMaker will recover automatically.
 If a program other than MemMaker starts after your computer
 restarts, exit the program so that MemMaker can continue.

    • Remove any disks from your floppy-disk drives and
      then press ENTER. Your computer will restart.




ENTER=Continue
```

10. Press Enter to restart your computer a second time.

11. After your computer reboots, another peculiar screen is displayed.

```
Microsoft MemMaker


   Your computer has just restarted with its new memory configuration.
   Some or all of your device drivers and memory-resident programs
   are now running in upper memory.

   If your system appears to be working properly, choose "Yes."
   If you noticed any unusual messages when your computer started,
   or if your system is not working properly, choose "No."

   Does your system appear to be working properly? Yes





ENTER=Accept Selection   SPACEBAR=Change Selection   F1=Help   F3=Exit
```

12. Does your computer *appear* to be working properly? If so, press Enter.

   MemMaker finally displays its last screen, in which it brags about how much it improved your memory configuration.

```
Microsoft MemMaker

MemMaker has finished optimizing your system's memory. The following
table summarizes the memory use (in bytes) on your system:

                              Before       After
  Memory Type                 MemMaker     MemMaker     Change

  Free conventional memory:   516,704      606,848      90,144

  Upper memory:
    Used by programs          156,416      174,064      17,648
    Reserved for Windows            0       24,576      24,576
    Reserved for EMS                0            0           0
    Free                        2,128       25,344

  Expanded memory:            Disabled     Disabled

Your original CONFIG.SYS and AUTOEXEC.BAT files have been saved
as CONFIG.UMB and AUTOEXEC.UMB.  If MemMaker changed your Windows
SYSTEM.INI file, the original file was saved as SYSTEM.UMB.

ENTER=Exit  ESC=Undo changes
```

13. Review the statistics shown on the MemMaker brag screen, especially the amount of conventional memory available before and after running MemMaker. When you're satisfied, press Enter. You will at last be returned to the familiar MS-DOS prompt.

Optimizing Memory with MemMaker When Configuration Menus Are Used

Unfortunately, MemMaker doesn't get along well with CONFIG.SYS files that define configuration menus. If you have defined multiple configurations in your CONFIG.SYS file, you should follow this procedure if you want to optimize your memory with MemMaker.

How to do it

1. Make a copy of your CONFIG.SYS and AUTOEXEC.BAT files for each configuration menu option you have. For example, if you have three configuration menu options, use the following commands to create three copies of CONFIG.SYS and AUTOEXEC.BAT:

   copy config.sys config.1

   copy config.sys config.2

copy config.sys config.3

copy autoexec.bat autoexec.1

copy autoexec.bat autoexec.2

copy autoexec.bat autoexec.3

2. Rename your original CONFIG.SYS and AUTOEXEC.BAT files using an extension other than UMB or BAK:

   rename config.sys config.sav

   rename autoexec.bat autoexec.sav

3. Edit each copy of your CONFIG.SYS file, removing all lines that don't pertain to the copy's configuration option. For example, remove all lines in the [menu] block and in unrelated configuration blocks. Be sure to account for lines in any [common] blocks.

4. Similarly edit each copy of your AUTOEXEC.BAT file.

5. Rename your first set of configuration files as follows:

   rename config.1 config.sys

   rename autoexec.1 autoexec.bat

6. Reboot your computer by pressing Ctrl-Alt-Delete.

7. Run MemMaker and follow the previous procedure outlined in "Optimizing Memory with MemMaker's Express Setup Mode" or "Optimizing Memory with MemMaker's Custom Setup Mode."

8. Rename the configuration files back to their original filenames:

   rename config.sys config.1

   rename autoexec.bat autoexec.1

9. Repeat steps 5 through 8 for each set of configuration files.

10. Now use the EDIT command to combine the separate configuration files back into a single set of CONFIG.SYS and AUTOEXEC.BAT files using your original configuration files as a guide.

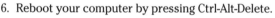

Undoing MemMaker's Changes

MemMaker makes some rather drastic changes to your CONFIG.SYS and AUTOEXEC.BAT files. If for any reason you decide you don't like what MemMaker has done, just undo it.

How to do it

1. Type the following command at the MS-DOS prompt:

   memmaker /undo

   The following screen will be displayed:

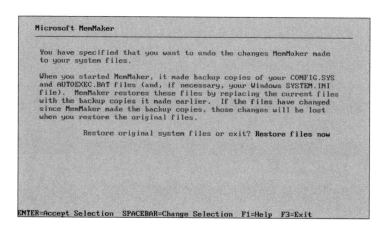

2. Select the "Restore files now" option by pressing Enter. The following screen is displayed:

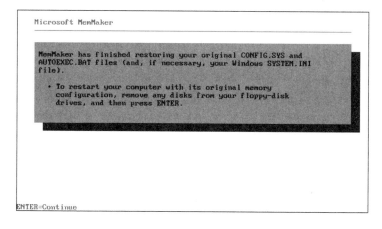

3. Press Enter to restart your computer using your original configuration files.

Multiple Configurations

If you find that you just can't decide among two or three memory configurations, you'll appreciate the multiple configuration feature available with MS-DOS 6.0 or later. It lets you set up a menu that is displayed when you start your computer. From this menu, you can pick the configuration you want to use. The following procedures show how to set up and use these configuration menus.

Creating a Config Menu

The procedure described here walks you through the process of creating a CONFIG.SYS file that displays a configuration menu when you start your computer.

How to do it quickly

Add the following lines to CONFIG.SYS:

[menu]	Marks the beginning of the menu section, which contains one or more **menuitem** commands
menuitem= *text*	Creates a menu choice (replace *text* with the name of the configuration block that will be processed if the user selects this choice)
[text]	Marks the beginning of a section that contains configuration commands for the corresponding menu choice
[common]	Marks the beginning of a section that contains configuration commands that are processed no matter which menu item is chosen

How to do it

1. Exit Windows if Windows is running (File⇨Exit). This procedure should be carried out from an MS-DOS prompt with Windows not running.

2. Type the following command:

   edit c:\config.sys

3. Add a [menu] section at the top of the CONFIG.SYS file. The [menu] section consists of the text **[menu]** on one line, followed by a **menuitem=*text*** line for each configuration option you want to appear on the menu. For example, the following [menu] section includes two menu options: one to start the computer normally ("Normal") and the other to start the computer with the MS-DOS 6.0 INTERLNK command enabled ("Interlnk").

```
[menu]
menuitem=Normal
menuitem=Interlnk
```

The text following **menuitem=** must be a single word with no intervening spaces.

4. After the [menu] section, place any CONFIG.SYS lines that are to be processed (no matter which menu option the user picks) following a [common] section. For example,

```
[common]
device=c:\dos\himem.sys
device=c:\dos\emm386.exe noems
dos=high
dos=umb
shell=c:\dos\command.com c:\dos\ /p
files=30
```

5. Place any commands that should be processed only if the user picks a particular option after a section marked by a [*menuitem-text*] line. For example, to load the INTERLNK.EXE driver if the user picks the Interlnk configuration, use these lines:

```
[Interlnk]
device=c:\dos\interlnk.exe
```

6. Insert the following line as the last line in your CONFIG.SYS file:

```
[common]
```

The CONFIG.SYS file shows what all these pieces look like when put together:

```
File  Edit  Search  Options                                          Help
                                    CONFIG.SYS
[menu]
menuitem=Normal
menuitem=Interlnk

[common]
device=c:\dos\himem.sys
device=c:\dos\emm386.exe noems
dos=high
dos=umb
shell=c:\dos\command.com c:\dos\ p:
files=30

[Interlnk]
device=c:\dos\interlnk.exe

[common]


MS-DOS Editor  <F1=Help> Press ALT to activate menus
```

7. Choose File⇨Save to save your changes.

8. Choose File⇨Exit to return to the MS-DOS prompt.

9. Press Ctrl-Alt-Delete to reboot your computer.

10. Applaud when MS-DOS displays the configuration menu.

```
MS-DOS 6.22 Startup Menu

    1. Normal
    2. Interlnk

Enter a choice: 1







F5=Bypass startup files F8=Confirm each line of CONFIG.SYS and AUTOEXEC.BAT [N]
```

11. Press the number corresponding to the configuration you want to use.

12. Carefully watch the messages that are displayed as your computer boots to make sure that all configuration commands are processed correctly. If necessary, use the MEM command to confirm that the correct device drivers have been loaded into memory.

13. Repeat steps 9–12 for each option on the configuration menu.

More stuff

Do not attempt to use MemMaker with a CONFIG.SYS file that includes a configuration menu; MemMaker doesn't know how to deal with the menu configuration commands. If you want to use MemMaker with configuration menus, you must first create a separate CONFIG.SYS file for each configuration menu option, run MemMaker separately on each CONFIG.SYS file, and then manually recombine the separate files into a single file. While you're at it, see if you can get your in-laws back on speaking terms, create a true spirit of bipartisanship in the House of Representatives, and get the members of the River City School Board to stop bickering.

Specifying a Time Out Default

You can instruct MS-DOS to automatically choose one of the config menu options if the user doesn't choose an option within a certain time period, such as five seconds.

How to do it quickly

Add the following line to the [menu] section of CONFIG.SYS:

menudefault=*text,time-out*

Replace *text* with the name of the default menu choice. Replace *time-out* with the number of seconds you want MS-DOS to wait before assuming the default choice.

How to do it

1. If your CONFIG.SYS file doesn't already have a configuration menu set up, follow the preceding procedure, "Creating a Config Menu," before continuing.

2. Edit the CONFIG.SYS file by typing this command at the MS-DOS prompt:

   edit c:\config.sys

3. Insert a line similar to the following line at the end of the [menu] section:

   menudefault=Normal,5

   This example tells MS-DOS to choose the "Normal" menu option if the user doesn't choose an option within five seconds.

   The CONFIG.SYS file shows the proper location for the **menudefault** line.

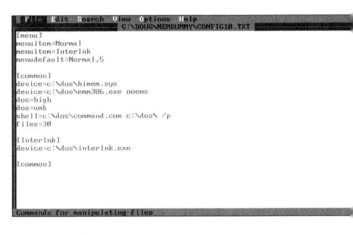

```
  File  Edit  Search  View  Options  Help
                    G:\DOUG\MEMDUMMY\CONFIG10.TXT
[menu]
menuitem=Normal
menuitem=Interlnk
menudefault=Normal,5

[common]
device=c:\dos\himem.sys
device=c:\dos\emm386.exe noems
dos=high
dos=umb
shell=c:\dos\command.com c:\dos\ /p
files=30

[Interlnk]
device=c:\dos\interlnk.exe

[common]




Commands for manipulating files
```

4. Choose File⇨Save to save your changes.

5. Choose File⇨Exit to return to the MS-DOS prompt.

6. Press Ctrl-Alt-Delete to reboot your computer.

7. The configuration menu appears, this time with a clock that counts down the seconds remaining before the default choice is taken.

8. Don't touch anything. Make sure that the correct configuration is taken when the countdown reaches zero.

```
MS-DOS 6.22 Startup Menu
═══════════════════════

   1. Normal
   2. Interlnk

Enter a choice: 1          Time remaining: 05








F5=Bypass startup files F8=Confirm each line of CONFIG.SYS and AUTOEXEC.BAT [N]
```

Setting Menu Colors

Tired of bland, white-on-black configuration menus? Follow this procedure to add color to your otherwise dreary computing life.

How to do it quickly

Add the following line to the [menu] section of CONFIG.SYS:

```
menucolor=text-color,background-color
```

Replace *text-color* with the number that corresponds to the color you want to use for menu text. Replace *background-color* with the number that corresponds to the color you want to use for the menu background. The colors represented by each number are shown in the table "Menu colors."

How to do it

1. Exit Windows if Windows is running (File⇨Exit). Windows is more colorful than DOS, but this procedure should be carried out from an MS-DOS prompt with Windows not running.

2. Type the following command:

   edit c:\config.sys

3. Insert a line similar to the following line at the end of the [menu] section:

```
menucolor=15,1
```

The first number represents the color of the text displayed for the menu; the second number represents the color of the menu background. Choose the numbers from the following table:

Number	Color	Number	Color
0	Black	8	Gray
1	Blue	9	Bright blue
2	Green	10	Bright green
3	Cyan	11	Bright cyan
4	Red	12	Bright red
5	Magenta	13	Bright magenta
6	Brown	14	Yellow
7	White	15	Bright white

The CONFIG.SYS file includes a **menucolor** line.

4. Choose File⇨Save to save your changes.
5. Choose File⇨Exit to return to the MS-DOS prompt.

6. Press Ctrl-Alt-Delete to reboot your computer.
7. The configuration menu appears, this time in living color (this menu looks much better in color).

```
MS-DOS 6.22 Startup Menu

   1. Normal
   2. InterInk

Enter a choice: 1        Time remaining: 05




F5=Bypass startup files F8=Confirm each line of CONFIG.SYS and AUTOEXEC.BAT [N]
```

Testing the Menu Choice in AUTOEXEC.BAT

When you use a configuration menu, MS-DOS sets an environment variable named CONFIG to indicate which configuration option you choose. You can use this environment variable to process different AUTOEXEC.BAT commands depending on which configuration option you choose.

How to do it quickly

Add the following line to your AUTOEXEC.BAT file:

```
goto %config%
```

Then add a label for each menuitem command that appears in your CONFIG.SYS file.

How to do it

1. Exit Windows if Windows is running (File⇨Exit). This isn't a Windows kind of thing.

2. Type the following command:

   edit c:\autoexec.bat

3. In the AUTOEXEC.BAT file, place any commands that should be executed regardless of which configuration option you chose at the beginning of the file. This would

most likely include such commands as PROMPT, PATH, SMARTDRV, and so on.

4. After the group of commands that are processed for all configurations, insert the following command:

```
goto %config%
```

5. Add the following label as the very last line in your AUTOEXEC.BAT file:

```
:end
```

6. Add a label for each menuitem line you placed in the [menu] section of your CONFIG.SYS file. Each label should be spelled exactly as it was spelled in the corresponding menuitem line, except that it should be preceded with a colon. After each label, insert the command **goto end**. For example,

```
:Normal
goto end
:Interlnk
goto end
```

7. Insert any commands you want carried out for a configuration between that configuration's label and the following goto end command. For example, to execute the command intersvr for the Interlnk configuration, insert the command as follows:

```
:Normal
goto end
:Interlnk
intersvr
goto end)
```

8. Choose File⇨Save to save your changes.

9. Choose File⇨Exit to return to the MS-DOS prompt.

10. Press Ctrl-Alt-Delete to reboot your computer.

```
 File  Edit  Search  Options                              Help
                            AUTOEXEC.BAT
prompt $p$g
path c:\dos;c:\windows;c:\util
smartdrv
goto %config%
:Normal
goto end
:Interlnk
intersvr
goto end
:end




MS-DOS Editor  <F1=Help> Press ALT to activate menus      N 00001:001
```

11. Pick a configuration option and watch as the CONFIG.SYS and AUTOEXEC.BAT files are processed to ensure that the correct commands are executed.

12. Repeat steps 10–11 for each configuration menu option.

RAM Drive

A RAM drive uses extended memory to simulate an additional disk drive. The following procedures show you how to set up and use a RAM drive.

RAM Drive

A simulated disk drive that uses extended or expanded memory instead of actual disk storage. Because RAM memory is much faster than disk storage, data can be read to and written to a RAM drive much faster than a real disk drive. However, any data in a RAM drive is permanently lost when you turn your computer off or reboot it. As a result, critical information such as data files should not be stored on a RAM drive.

Creating a RAM Drive

You can create a RAM drive by using extended memory.

How to do it quickly

Add the following line to your CONFIG.SYS file:

```
devicehigh=c:\dos\ramdrive.sys size /e
```

Replace *size* with the size (in K) of the RAM drive you want to create.

How to do it

1. Exit Windows if Windows is running (File➪Exit). This procedure must be performed from an MS-DOS prompt.

2. Type the following command:

   edit c:\config.sys

3. Add the following line to your CONFIG.SYS file:

   ```
   devicehigh=c:\dos\ramdrive.sys 1024 /e
   ```

   This creates a 1MB RAM drive. (Actually, it creates a 1024K RAM drive, but 1024K happens to be the same as 1MB. If you don't want to create such a large RAM drive, type a different number in place of 1024.) The line can be placed anywhere after the **device=c:\dos\himem.sys** and **device=c:\dos\emm386.exe** lines.

   The CONFIG.SYS file shows the proper placement of the **device=c:\dos\ramdrive.sys** line.

4. Choose File➪Save to save your changes.

5. Choose File➪Exit to return to the MS-DOS prompt.

6. Press Ctrl-Alt-Delete to reboot your computer. As your computer boots, watch the messages that are displayed. One of the messages tells you which drive letter has been assigned to the RAM drive:

```
   File  Edit  Search  View  Options  Help
                      G:\DOUG\MEMDUMMY\CONFIG12.TXT
device=c:\dos\himem.sys
device=c:\dos\emm386.exe noems
dos=high
dos=umb
devicehigh=c:\dos\ramdrive.sys 1024 /e
shell=c:\dos\command.com c:\dos\ /p
files=30




F1=Help                                          Line:6    Col:36
```

```
Microsoft RAMDrive Version 3.07 virtual
disk D:
Disk size: 1024k
Sector size: 512 bytes
Allocation unit: 1 sectors
Directory entries: 64
```

Here, the RAM drive has been assigned drive letter D. Your mileage may vary.

7. To verify that the RAM drive was created properly, type this command (vary the drive letter as needed):

   dir d:

You should get a display similar to this one:

```
Volume in drive D is MS-RAMDRIVE
Directory of D:\

File not found
```

I hope you don't get something like this:

```
Invalid drive specification
```

If you do, something didn't work. Double-check your
CONFIG.SYS file and make sure that you have enough
extended memory to create the RAM drive.

More stuff

You can use expanded memory to create a RAM drive. Replace
the /e at the end of the RAMDRIVE.SYS line with **/a**, like so:

```
devicehigh=c:\dos\ramdrive.sys 1024 /a
```

Do this only if you have an actual expanded memory card. It's
inefficient to use extended memory to simulate expanded memory.
Then create a RAM drive using the simulated expanded memory. It's
better to dispense with the simulated expanded memory altogether
and create the RAM drive from true-blue extended memory.

You can also create a RAM drive from regular conventional
memory, but it's not a good idea. If your computer has no
extended or expanded memory, you probably have more
important uses for your precious conventional memory.

Copying Files to a RAM Drive

After you create a RAM drive, what should you do with it? Copy
some files to it, of course! Which files, you ask? Why, the ones
that benefit the most from being in a RAM drive. These might
include your batch files or perhaps your favorite utility programs.
Either way, the following procedure shows you how to get these
files copied to your RAM drive automatically whenever you start
your computer.

How to do it quickly

Add an XCOPY command similar to the following to your
AUTOEXEC.BAT file:

```
xcopy c:\bat\*.* d:
```

Substitute the directory you want to copy to the RAM drive and
the drive letter assigned to your RAM drive if necessary.

1. Exit Windows if Windows is running. This procedure must
   be performed from an MS-DOS prompt.

2. Type the following command:

   edit c:\autoexec.bat

3. Add the commands necessary to copy the files you want stored on the RAM drive to your AUTOEXEC.BAT file. For example:

```
xcopy c:\bat\*.bat d:
```

   This command copies all batch files in the C:\BAT directory to the RAM drive. The command can be placed anywhere in the AUTOEXEC.BAT file.

4. Adjust the PATH command in your AUTOEXEC.BAT file so that it includes the root directory of your RAM drive:

```
path d:\;c:\dos;c:\windows;c:\winword;c:\excel
```

   Notice that the RAM drive appears first on the PATH command.

5. If your RAM drive is large enough (512K or more), add this command to your AUTOEXEC.BAT file:

```
set temp=d:\
```

   This tells MS-DOS to create temporary files on the RAM drive, assuming that the RAM drive is assigned drive letter D.

   The following sample AUTOEXEC.BAT file shows the proper placement of these commands:

```
File  Edit  Search  Options                                        Help
╒══════════════════════════ AUTOEXEC.BAT ══════════════════════════╕
@echo off
prompt $p$g
lh c:\dos\mscdex.exe /e:mscd001 /s /l:e
lh c:\dos\smartdrv.exe
path d:\;c:\dos;c:\windows;c:\winword;c:\excel
xcopy c:\bat\*.* d:
set temp=d:
win




MS-DOS Editor  <F1=Help> Press ALT to activate menus                N 00001:001
```

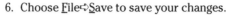

6. Choose File⇨Save to save your changes.

7. Choose File⇨Exit to return to the MS-DOS prompt.

8. Press Ctrl-Alt-Delete to reboot your computer.

SmartDrive

The procedures in this section show you how to activate and use the MS-DOS SmartDrive command, which boosts the speed of your disk drives. SmartDrive works its magic by setting up a *disk cache,* which unfortunately requires extended or expanded memory. If you have the memory to spare, however, SmartDrive is a miracle worker.

Disk Cache

An area of extended or expanded memory that is used to hold data that would otherwise have to be read from or written to a disk drive. Because extended or expanded memory is much faster than disk storage, using a disk cache can make your computer run significantly faster. *Cache* is pronounced like *cash,* which should be a $400 *Jeopardy* answer.

Activating SmartDrive

Activating SmartDrive is as easy as inserting a command in your AUTOEXEC.BAT file.

How to do it quickly

Add the following line to your AUTOEXEC.BAT file:

```
lh c:\dos\smartdrv.exe
```

How to do it

1. Exit Windows if Windows is running (File⇨Exit). This procedure must be performed from an MS-DOS prompt.

2. Type the following command:

   edit c:\autoexec.bat

3. Check to see if a SMARTDRV command is already present in your AUTOEXEC.BAT file. It may be a simple command such as this:

```
smartdrv
```

Or it may be convoluted, like this:

```
lh /1:0;1,45488 /s c:\dos\smartdrv.exe 2048 1024
```

If you find a SMARTDRV command, SmartDrive is already installed. Choose File➪Exit and skip the rest of this procedure.

4. Insert the following command in your AUTOEXEC.BAT file:

```
lh c:\dos\smartdrv.exe
```

This command activates SmartDrive and loads it into upper memory if possible. (See the upper memory procedures that appear later in this section for more information about upper memory.)

The placement of the command isn't too important. Your computer will boot faster if you place the SMARTDRV command closer to the beginning of AUTOEXEC.BAT. If you have a CD-ROM drive, however, you should place the SMARTDRV command *after* the MSCDEX command.

The following sample AUTOEXEC.BAT file includes a SMARTDRV command.

```
File  Edit  Search  Options                                    Help
┌──────────────────────── AUTOEXEC.BAT ────────────────────────┐
@echo off
prompt $p$g
lh c:\dos\mscdex.exe /e:mscd001 /s /l:e
lh c:\dos\smartdrv.exe
path c:\dos;c:\windows;c:\winword;c:\excel
win




MS-DOS Editor  <F1=Help> Press ALT to activate menus            N 00001:001
```

5. Choose File⇨Save to save your changes.

 6. Choose File⇨Exit to return to the MS-DOS prompt.

7. Press Ctrl-Alt-Delete to reboot your computer.

More stuff

SmartDrive has a second function in addition to creating a disk cache: it provides an important feature called *double-buffering*, which is required to cajole certain unruly disk drives into behaving themselves. This double-buffering feature is activated by including a **device=c:\dos\smartdrv.exe /double_buffer** command in your CONFIG.SYS file. Mercifully, MS-DOS automatically adds this line to your CONFIG.SYS file if it determines that you have one of these miscreant disk drives attached to your computer, so you don't have to worry about it.

 If you want to, you can fiddle around with the amount of memory used for SmartDrive's cache. Refer to the description of the SMARTDRV command in Part IV of this book.

Caching CD-ROM Drives

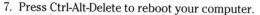 If you have MS-DOS 6.2 or 6.22, SmartDrive is able to cache CD-ROM drives as well as disk drives. This procedure ensures that caching is enabled for CD-ROM drives.

How to do it quickly

Make sure that the smartdrv command comes *after* the mscdex command in your AUTOEXEC.BAT file:

```
lh c:\dos\mscdex.exe /e:mscd001 /s /l:e
lh c:\dos\smartdrv.exe
```

How to do it

1. Exit Windows if Windows is running (File⇨Exit). This procedure must be performed from an MS-DOS prompt.

2. Type the following command:

   edit c:\autoexec.bat

3. Find the SMARTDRV command. It may be a simple command such as this:

```
smartdrv
```

Or it may be convoluted, like this:

```
lh /1:0;1,45488 /s c:\dos\smartdrv.exe 2048 1024
```

4. Find the MSCDEX command. It probably looks something like this:

```
mscdex /e:mscd001 /s /l:e
```

However, it may begin with LH or LOADHIGH, as in this example:

```
lh c:\dos\mscdex.exe /e:mscd001 /s /l:e
```

5. Here's the tricky part: Make sure that the MSCDEX command comes *before* the SMARTDRV command. If it does not, switch the commands.

The following sample AUTOEXEC.BAT file shows the proper placement of SMARTDRV and MSCDEX to ensure that CD-ROM drives are cached:

6. Choose File⇨Save to save your changes.

7. Choose File⇨Exit to return to the MS-DOS prompt.

8. Press Ctrl-Alt-Delete to reboot your computer.

Upper Memory

This section presents several procedures for activating and utilizing upper memory (that 384K chunk of memory that resides between 640K and 1MB).

Upper memory

A 384K area of memory that follows immediately after the 640K of conventional memory. On a 386 or better computer, upper memory can be used to hold programs that would otherwise consume conventional memory. This leaves more conventional memory available for DOS application programs.

Activating Upper Memory

You can activate upper memory so that MS-DOS can use it to hold programs that would otherwise chew up valuable conventional memory.

How to do it quickly

Add the following lines to CONFIG.SYS:

```
device=c:\dos\himem.sys
device=c:\dos\emm386.exe noems
dos=high
dos=umb
```

How to do it

1. Exit Windows if Windows is running (File⇨Exit). This procedure must be performed from an MS-DOS prompt.

2. Type the following command:

   edit c:\config.sys

3. If you are using MS-DOS 6.*x*, add the following lines at the top of the CONFIG.SYS file:

```
device=c:\dos\himem.sys
device=c:\dos\emm386.exe noems
```

   Also use the preceding lines if you have MS-DOS 5 and do *not* have Windows 3.1.

   If you use a version of MS-DOS earlier than 6.0 but you also use Windows 3.1, add these lines instead:

```
device=c:\windows\himem.sys
device=c:\windows\emm386.exe noems
```

   The trick is to use the newest available HIMEM.SYS and EMM386.EXE version, whether it resides in your \WINDOWS or \DOS directory.

4. Add the following line to your CONFIG.SYS file:

```
dos=umb
```

   It can appear anywhere after the line inserted in step 3. This command can also appear as:

```
dos=high,umb
```

   However, I recommend you keep **dos=high** and **dos=umb** on separate lines.

   The following sample CONFIG.SYS file includes the cmmands necessary to activate Upper Memory Blocks and enable MS-DOS support for UMBs:

5. Choose File⇨Save to save your changes.

6. Choose File⇨Exit to return to the MS-DOS prompt.

```
  File  Edit  Search  View  Options  Help
                       G:\DOUG\MEMDUMMY\CONFIG13.TXT
device=c:\dos\himem.sys
device=c:\dos\emm386.exe noems
dos=high
dos=umb
devicehigh=c:\dos\ansi.sys
devicehigh=c:\dos\setver.exe
shell=c:\dos\command.com c:\dos\ /p
files=30




F1=Help                                        Line:7    Col:36
```

7. Press Ctrl-Alt-Del to reboot your computer.

8. Run the MEM command to verify that upper memory is available.

More stuff

For more information about the **dos=high** command, see the procedure, "Loading DOS into the High Memory Area (HMA)," earlier in this part.

Loading a Device Driver into Upper Memory

After you enable upper memory (see the preceding procedure, "Activating Upper Memory"), loading a device driver into upper memory is easy.

How to do it quickly

Change the CONFIG.SYS **device** command that loads the driver to a **devicehigh** command:

```
devicehigh=c:\dos\ansi.sys
```

How to do it

1. Exit Windows if Windows is running (File⇨Exit). This procedure must be performed from an MS-DOS prompt.

2. Type the following command:

   edit c:\config.sys

3. Find the **device** command that names the driver you want to load into upper memory. For example,

   ```
   device=c:\dos\ansi.sys
   ```

4. Change it to a **devicehigh** command:

   ```
   devicehigh=c:\dos\ansi.sys
   ```

5. Repeat steps 3 and 4 for any other device drivers you want to move to upper memory. The only two device commands you should not change to **devicehigh** are the commands that load HIMEM.SYS and EMM386.EXE, as these are the commands that enable upper memory in the first place.

   The following CONFIG.SYS file shows how to load device drivers into upper memory:

The **devicehigh** command tries its hardest to load a device driver into upper memory. If there's no room at the inn, the driver is loaded into conventional memory as if you had used a **device** command instead of **devicehigh**.

6. Choose File⇨Save to save your changes.

7. Choose File⇨Exit to return to the MS-DOS prompt.

8. Press Ctrl-Alt-Del to reboot your computer.

9. Run the **mem /c** command to confirm that the driver has been loaded into upper memory. The driver should appear in the list of modules using memory below 1MB, and it should indicate that it is using upper memory rather than conventional memory. In the following example, you can see that the ANSI driver (ANSI.SYS) has been loaded into upper memory:

```
Modules using memory below 1 MB:

Name          Total      =   Conventional   +   Upper Memory
------------  --------  -----  -----------  -----  ----------  -----
MSDOS         17,021    (17K)    17,021     (17K)       0      (0K)
HIMEM          1,168     (1K)     1,168      (1K)       0      (0K)
EMM386         3,120     (3K)     3,120      (3K)       0      (0K)
COMMAND        3,184     (3K)     3,184      (3K)       0      (0K)
MSCDEX        28,288    (28K)    28,288     (28K)       0      (0K)
MOUSE         17,088    (17K)    17,088     (17K)       0      (0K)
MTMCDD        50,800    (50K)         0      (0K)   50,800    (50K)
DRVSPACE      39,840    (39K)         0      (0K)   39,840    (39K)
ANSI           4,272     (4K)         0      (0K)    4,272     (4K)
SMARTDRV      30,368    (30K)         0      (0K)   30,368    (30K)
SHARE         16,944    (17K)         0      (0K)   16,944    (17K)
Free         601,680   (588K)   585,296    (572K)   16,384    (16K)

Memory Summary:

Type of Memory     Total    =    Used     +    Free
-------------     -------       -------       -------
Conventional      655,360        70,064       585,296
Upper             158,608       142,224        16,384
Press any key to continue . . .
```

More stuff

For more information about the **device** command, see its entry in Part IV of this book.

Loading a Program into Upper Memory in AUTOEXEC.BAT

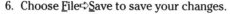

Having enabled upper memory (see the procedure, "Activating Upper Memory," earlier in this section), you can load any memory-resident program such as SMARTDRV or SHARE into upper memory.

How to do it quickly

In AUTOEXEC.BAT, add **lh** to the beginning of any memory-resident command you want loaded into upper memory. For example,

```
lh c:\dos\smartdrv
```

How to do it

1. Exit Windows if Windows is running (File⇨Exit). This procedure must be performed from an MS-DOS prompt.

2. Type the following command:

   edit c:\autoexec.bat

3. Find the command that loads the memory-resident program you want moved to upper memory. For example,

```
c:\dos\smartdrv
```

4. Add **lh** to the beginning of the command:

```
lh c:\dos\smartdrv
```

5. Repeat steps 3 and 4 for any other memory-resident programs you want to move to upper memory.

   The following AUTOEXEC.BAT file shows how to load memory-resident programs into upper memory:

```
                              AUTOEXEC.BAT
@echo off
prompt $p$g
lh c:\dos\mscdex.exe /e:mscd001 /s /l:e
lh c:\dos\smartdrv.exe
path c:\dos;c:\windows;c:\winword;c:\excel
win




MS-DOS Editor   <F1=Help> Press ALT to activate menus
```

The **lh** command tries its hardest to load a memory-resident program into upper memory. If the program won't fit, **lh** loads the program into conventional memory as usual.

6. Choose File⇨Save to save your changes.

7. Choose File⇨Exit to return to the MS-DOS prompt.

8. Press Ctrl-Alt-Delete to reboot your computer.

9. Run the **mem /c** command to confirm that the driver has been loaded into upper memory. The driver should appear in the list of modules using memory below 1MB, and it should indicate that it is using upper memory rather than conventional memory. In the following example, you can see that the ANSI driver (ANSI.SYS) has been loaded into upper memory:

```
Modules using memory below 1 MB:

Name          Total    =    Conventional  +   Upper Memory
------------------------------------------------------------
MSDOS        17,021   (17K)    17,021   (17K)        0    (0K)
HIMEM         1,168    (1K)     1,168    (1K)        0    (0K)
EMM386        3,120    (3K)     3,120    (3K)        0    (0K)
COMMAND       3,104    (3K)     3,104    (3K)        0    (0K)
MSCDEX       28,288   (28K)    28,288   (28K)        0    (0K)
MOUSE        17,088   (17K)    17,088   (17K)        0    (0K)
MTMCDD       50,800   (50K)         0    (0K)   50,800   (50K)
DRVSPACE     39,840   (39K)         0    (0K)   39,840   (39K)
ANSI          4,272    (4K)         0    (0K)    4,272    (4K)
SMARTDRV     30,368   (30K)         0    (0K)   30,368   (30K)
SHARE        16,944   (17K)         0    (0K)   16,944   (17K)
Free        601,680  (588K)   585,296  (572K)   16,384   (16K)

Memory Summary:

Type of Memory     Total    =    Used     +    Free
----------------------------------------------------------
Conventional      655,360         70,064       585,296
Upper             158,608        142,224        16,384
Press any key to continue . . .
```

More stuff

For more information about the **lh** command, see its entry in Part IV of this book.

Windows Memory Configuration

This section contains procedures that help you optimize memory use with Microsoft Windows 3.1.

Determining How Much Windows Memory Is Available

 Here's the quick way to find out how much memory is available to Windows and how much of those pesky Windows Resources have been consumed already.

How to do it quickly

From Program Manager or File Manager, call up the Help⇨About command.

How to do it

1. Switch to Program Manager or File Manager.

2. Choose Help⇨About command. This brings up the About dialog box. Here's what it looks like in Program Manager:

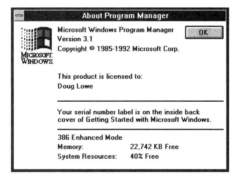

3. Note the amount of memory that is free. In the preceding example, 22,742K (about 22MB) is free. Note that this amount includes extended memory plus the Windows swap file.

4. Next notice the amount of System Resources that are free. In the above example, only 40% System Resources are available. Weird things start to happen in Windows when this figure drops below 10%.

5. Click OK when you've seen enough.

 This procedure also works from the Windows accessories, such as Write or Paintbrush.

Creating a Permanent Swap File

One of the best ways to make Windows use memory more efficiently is to create a permanent swap file.

How to do it quickly

Open the Control Panel; then double-click the 386 Enhanced icon. Click the Virtual Memory button and then the Change button. Select Permanent from the Type drop-down box; then type the size of the swap file in the New Size box. Click the OK button, then click Yes to make the changes, and then click Restart Now to restart Windows so the changes take effect.

How to do it

1. Exit from any programs you are running. This procedure should be run from Windows with no other programs running.

2. From Program Manager, open the Main group if it is not already open:

3. Double-click the Control Panel icon. Control Panel appears.

4. Double-click the 386 Enhanced icon in Control Panel. The 386 Enhanced dialog box appears:

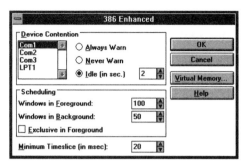

5. Click the Virtual Memory button. The Virtual Memory dialog box appears:

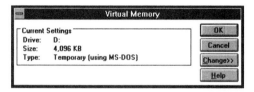

6. Click the Change>> button. The dialog box expands, revealing the secret that allows you to change the virtual memory settings.

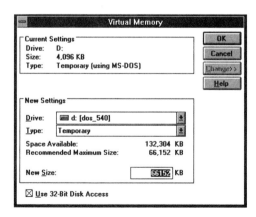

7. Change the Type drop-down list to Permanent and type a reasonable number (such as 4096 or 8192) for the New Size field. For example,

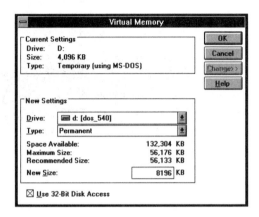

8. If you should happen to type a New Size that's larger than the recommended size, you'll get the following bogus dialog box:

Windows is lying here. It actually will use whatever size you type, even if it is larger than the recommended size. Click OK.

9. The following dialog box appears, which is the polite way Windows has of saying, "Do you know what you're doing?"

10. Click Yes. Yet another dialog box appears:

Click on the Restart Windows button. Get a cup of coffee while Windows restarts itself.

11. When the familiar Program Manager appears, you're done. Whew!

Removing TrueType Fonts to Conserve Memory

If you encounter an "insufficient memory" message while using a Windows application, you can sometimes alleviate the problem by removing TrueType fonts you don't use to free up Windows resource memory (whatever that is).

If you get an "insufficient memory" message, don't switch to File Manager and start deleting files in an effort to free up memory. The message refers to insufficient RAM; deleting files frees up disk space but doesn't free up the needed RAM. Remember: memory and disk storage are two different things.

How to do it quickly

Open the Control Panel; then double-click the Fonts icon. Select a font you don't use; then click Remove. Click Yes to confirm that you want to remove the font.

How to do it

1. From Program Manager, open the Main group if it is not already open.

2. Double-click the Control Panel icon. Control Panel appears.

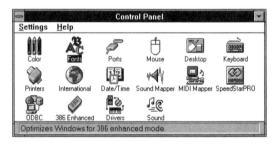

3. Double-click the Fonts icon in Control Panel. The Fonts dialog box appears.

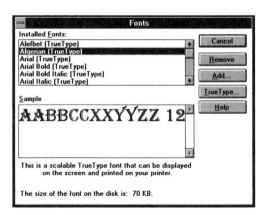

4. Click a font you don't need; then click on the Remove button. A confirmation dialog box appears.

5. Click OK. Leave the Delete Font File From Disk option unchecked. The font will be removed from the list but will remain on your hard disk. (If you decide you need the font back, you can click the Add button in the Fonts dialog box.)

 Make sure you don't delete a font that you use. If you open a document that was formatted with a font you've since deleted, Windows will substitute something boring like Times New Roman. Yuck!

6. Repeat steps 4 and 5 for other fonts you want to remove.

7. Click the Close button when you're done. Change the Type drop-down list to Permanent, and type a reasonable number (such as 4096 or 8192) for the New Size field.

8. You're done.

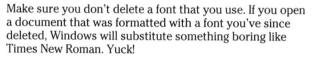

Removing Wallpaper to Conserve Memory

Wallpaper is a notorious consumer of Windows memory. If you start getting "insufficient memory" messages while running Windows applications, removing your wallpaper might help alleviate the problem.

 If you get an "insufficient memory" message, don't switch to File Manager and start deleting files in an effort to free up memory. The message refers to insufficient RAM; deleting files frees up disk space but doesn't free up the needed RAM. Remember: memory and disk storage are two different things.

How to do it quickly

Open the Control Panel; then double-click the Desktop icon. Change the Wallpaper File setting to None and then click OK.

How to do it

1. From Program Manager, open the Main group if it is not already open.

2. Double-click the Control Panel icon. Control Panel will appear.

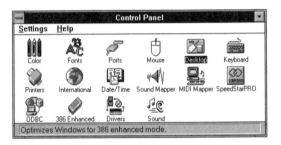

3. Double-click the Desktop icon in Control Panel. The Desktop dialog box will appear.

4. Change the Wallpaper File field to (None):

5. Click OK. You're done!

Changing Video Mode to Conserve Memory

Although many computers sold today can display 65 thousand or even 16 million different colors with a resolution of 800 x 600 or 1,024 x 768, you can save a substantial amount of memory by configuring your monitor to use fewer colors and lower resolution. For example, switching from 800 x 600 at 65,000 colors to 640 x 480 with 256 colors frees up about 183K of Windows memory for other uses.

How to do it quickly

Run Windows Setup from the Main group. Select the Options⇨Change System Settings command; then change the Display drop-down list to an option with less resolution than the current display setting. Click OK.

How to do it

1. Exit any programs that might be running under Windows. This is the kind of thing that shouldn't be attempted while other programs are running.

2. From Program Manager, open the Main group if it is not already open.

3. Double-click the Windows Setup icon. Windows Setup will appear.

4. Choose Options⇨Change System Settings. The Change System Settings dialog box appears.

5. Use the Display drop-down list to display a display driver that has lower resolution or fewer colors (or both) than the current driver. For example,

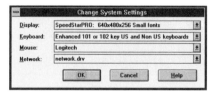

6. Click on OK. A confirmation dialog box appears.

7. Click on Current. (If you are asked to insert one of the Windows installation diskettes, do so.) After the driver has been installed, the Exit Windows Setup dialog box appears.

8. Click Restart Windows to restart Windows and activate the new driver. You're done!

Part III
CONFIG.SYS and AUTOEXEC.BAT Files You Can Copy

This part of the book contains a bevy of CONFIG.SYS and AUTOEXEC.BAT files you can copy verbatim. Well, almost verbatim. Unfortunately, there are just too many variations in computer hardware and software to summarize in a half dozen or so examples, so you'll have to think of the configurations presented in this part as starting points. Find the one configuration that comes closest to matching your computer's configuration and your software and then tailor it to suit your needs.

All of the examples in this chapter assume that you are using MS-DOS 6.22. Adjustments may be necessary for earlier versions of MS-DOS, particularly versions prior to 5.0.

8088/8086 Computer with an Expanded Memory Card

Unfortunately, memory management is a difficult proposition for 8088 and 8086 computers. About the only option is adding additional memory by installing an expanded memory card into the computer. Then, you must include a **device** command in your CONFIG.SYS file to make the memory usable. The following configuration files assume that you have 1MB expanded memory installed on the computer.

CONFIG.SYS

```
device=c:\intel\emm.sys pc e000 208
device=c:\dos\ramdrive.sys 512 /a
device=c:\dos\ansi.sys
buffers=10
files=30
shell=c:\dos\command.com c:\dos\ /e:512 /p
```

AUTOEXEC.BAT

```
@echo off
prompt $p$g
path c:\dos;c:\123;c:\util
```

Notes

The **device=c:\intel\emm.sys** command in the CONFIG.SYS file names EMM.SYS as the device driver that activates the expanded memory card. This driver, which is provided along with the expanded memory card, is not a part of MS-DOS and may be given a name other than EMM.SYS. Read the instructions that come with the memory card to be sure that the driver is configured properly.

The **device=c:\dos\ramdrive.sys** command in the CONFIG.SYS file creates a RAM drive using half of the available expanded memory (512K). If you don't need a RAM drive, omit this line.

 The **device=c:\dos\ansi.sys** command in the CONFIG.SYS file activates the ANSI.SYS display driver, which lets you create fancy screen displays. Omit this line if you don't use any programs that require a fancy screen display. See RAM drive proceedures in Part II for more information.

 The buffers, files, and shell lines also consume valuable memory. See the entries for these commands in Part IV for more information.

You can't do much else to improve memory use on the 8088 computer. Maybe it's time to get a new one. . . .

80286 Computer Running MS-DOS Only

The following configuration files assume that you have the 80286 computer with 384K of extended memory and a 1MB expanded memory card. The files take advantage of the 80286 computer's ability to utilize extended memory for a disk cache and to load DOS into the high memory area.

CONFIG.SYS

```
device=c:\dos\himem.sys
dos=high
device=c:\intel\emm.sys pc e000 208
device=c:\dos\ramdrive.sys 512 /a
device=c:\dos\ansi.sys
buffers=10
files=30
shell=c:\dos\command.com c:\dos\ /e:512 /p
```

AUTOEXEC.BAT

```
@echo off
prompt $p$g
path c:\dos;c:\123;c:\util
c:\dos\smartdrv.exe
```

Notes

The **device=c:\dos\himem.sys** command in the CONFIG.SYS file activates extended memory. The **dos=high** command stuffs part of MS-DOS into the first 64K of extended memory, which is often called the high memory area (HMA).

The **device=c:\intel\emm.sys** command in the CONFIG.SYS file names EMM.SYS as the device driver that activates the expanded memory card. This driver, which is provided along with the expanded memory card, is not part of MS-DOS and may be given a name other than EMM.SYS. Read the instructions that come with the memory card to be sure that the driver is configured properly. If you don't have an expanded memory card installed in your computer, omit this line.

The **device=c:\dos\ramdrive.sys** command in the CONFIG.SYS file creates a RAM drive using half of the available expanded memory (512K). If you don't need a RAM drive, omit this line.

The **device=c:\dos\ansi.sys** command in the CONFIG.SYS file activates the ANSI.SYS display driver, which lets you create fancy screen displays. Omit this line if you don't use any programs that require fancy screen displays.

The **c:\dos\smartdrv.exe** command in the AUTOEXEC.BAT file creates a disk cache using the 80286 computer's extended memory.

80286 Computer Foolishly Running Windows

Windows runs poorly on the 80286 computer, but it will run if you have at least 1MB of memory. Of course, the more extended memory you can provide, the better the performance. For adequate performance, make sure that your computer has at least 4MB of memory.

CONFIG.SYS

```
device=c:\dos\himem.sys
device=c:\intel\emm.sys at e000 208
dos=high
buffers=10
files=30
shell=c:\dos\command.com c:\dos\ /e:512 /p
```

AUTOEXEC.BAT

```
@echo off
prompt $p$g
path c:\windows;c:\dos;c:\123;c:\util
c:\dos\smartdrv.exe
win
```

Notes

The **device=c:\dos\himem.sys** command in the CONFIG.SYS file activates extended memory. The **dos=high** command stuffs part of MS-DOS into the first 64K of extended memory, which is often called the high memory area (HMA).

The **device=c:\intel\emm.sys** command in the CONFIG.SYS file
names EMM.SYS as the device driver that activates expanded
memory. This driver, which is provided along with the expanded
memory card, is not part of MS-DOS and may be given a name
other than EMM.SYS. Read the instructions that came with the
memory card to be sure that the driver is configured properly. If
you don't have an expanded memory card installed in your
computer, or if you don't want to provide any expanded memory
for MS-DOS programs, omit this line.

The **c:\dos\smartdrv.exe** command in the AUTOEXEC.BAT file
creates a disk cache using the 80286 computer's extended
memory.

The **win** command in the AUTOEXEC.BAT file starts Windows.

386 or Better Computer Running MS-DOS Only and Requiring EMS Memory

Here are configuration files for a 386 or better computer that runs
only MS-DOS applications (no Windows-based applications),
which require expanded memory.

CONFIG.SYS

```
device=c:\dos\himem.sys
device=c:\dos\emm386.exe ram
dos=high
dos=umb
devicehigh=c:\dos\ansi.sys
buffers=10
files=30
shell=c:\dos\command.com c:\dos\ /e:512 /p
```

AUTOEXEC.BAT

```
@echo off
prompt $p$g
path c:\dos;c:\123;c:\util
c:\dos\smartdrv.exe
```

Notes

The **device=c:\dos\himem.sys** command in the CONFIG.SYS file activates extended memory. The **dos=high** command stuffs part of MS-DOS into the first 64K of extended memory, which is often called the high memory area (HMA).

The **device=c:\dos\emm386.exe ram** command in the CONFIG.SYS file activates upper memory and expanded memory. The **dos=umb** command that appears later instructs DOS to allow programs and drivers to be loaded into upper memory. See the entries for these commands in Part IV for more information.

The **devicehigh=c:\dos\ansi.sys** command in the CONFIG.SYS file activates the ANSI.SYS display driver, which lets you create fancy screen displays. Omit this line if you don't use any programs that require fancy displays produced by ANSI.SYS.

The **c:\dos\smartdrv.exe** command in the AUTOEXEC.BAT file creates a disk cache using the computer's extended memory.

---

386 or Better Computer Running MS-DOS Only With No EMS Memory Required

Here are configuration files for the 386 or better computer that runs only MS-DOS applications (no Windows-based applications), which do not require expanded memory. Assume that the computer has 4MB of memory.

CONFIG.SYS

```
device=c:\dos\himem.sys
device=c:\dos\emm386.exe noems
dos=high
dos=umb
devicehigh=c:\dos\ansi.sys
buffers=10
files=30
shell=c:\dos\command.com c:\dos\ /e:512 /p
```

AUTOEXEC.BAT

```
@echo off
prompt $p$g
path c:\dos;c:\123;c:\util
c:\dos\smartdrv.exe
```

Notes

The **device=c:\dos\himem.sys** command in the CONFIG.SYS file activates extended memory. The **dos=high** command stuffs part of MS-DOS into the first 64K of extended memory, which is often called the high memory area (HMA).

The **device=c:\dos\emm386.exe noems** command in the CONFIG.SYS file activates upper memory. The **dos=umb** command that appears later instructs DOS to allow programs and drivers to be loaded into upper memory.

The **devicehigh=c:\dos\ansi.sys** command in the CONFIG.SYS file activates the ANSI.SYS display driver, which lets you create fancy screen displays. Omit this line if you don't use any programs that require it.

The **c:\dos\smartdrv.exe** command in the AUTOEXEC.BAT file creates a disk cache using the computer's extended memory.

386 or Better Computer Running Windows

Here are configuration files for a 386 or better computer that runs Windows. Assume that the computer has at least 4MB of memory.

CONFIG.SYS

```
device=c:\dos\himem.sys
device=c:\dos\emm386.exe noems
dos=high
dos=umb
buffers=10
files=30
shell=c:\dos\command.com c:\dos\ /e:512 /p
```

AUTOEXEC.BAT

```
@echo off
prompt $p$g
path c:\windows;c:\dos;c:\123;c:\util
c:\dos\smartdrv.exe
win
```

Notes

The **device=c:\dos\himem.sys** command in the CONFIG.SYS file activates extended memory. The **dos=high** command stuffs part of MS-DOS into the first 64K of extended memory, which is often called the high memory area (HMA).

The **device=c:\dos\emm386.exe noems** command in the CONFIG.SYS file activates upper memory. The **dos=umb** command that appears later instructs DOS to allow programs and drivers to be loaded into upper memory.

The **c:\dos\smartdrv.exe** command in the AUTOEXEC.BAT file creates a disk cache using the computer's extended memory.

The **win** command in the AUTOEXEC.BAT file starts Windows.

386 or Better Computer Running Windows for Workgroups 3.11 Using 32-Bit File Access

Here are configuration files for a 386 or better computer running Windows for Workgroups with 32-bit File Access enabled. Assume that the computer has at least 4MB of memory.

CONFIG.SYS

```
device=c:\dos\himem.sys
device=c:\dos\emm386.exe noems
dos=high
dos=umb
buffers=10
files=30
shell=c:\dos\command.com c:\dos\ /e:512 /p
```

AUTOEXEC.BAT

```
@echo off
prompt $p$g
path c:\windows;c:\dos;c:\123;c:\util
win
```

Notes

The **device=c:\dos\himem.sys** command in the CONFIG.SYS file activates extended memory. The **dos=high** command stuffs part of MS-DOS into the first 64K of extended memory, which is often called the high memory area (HMA).

The **device=c:\dos\emm386.exe noems** command in the CONFIG.SYS file activates upper memory. The **dos=umb** command that appears later instructs DOS to allow programs and drivers to be loaded into upper memory.

The **win** command in the AUTOEXEC.BAT file starts Windows. Notice that the AUTOEXEC.BAT file does *not* run the SmartDrive disk cache. Since 32-bit file access provides its own form of disk caching, SmartDrive is not required. (If you run MS-DOS applications in addition to Windows applications, include a SMARTDRV command in AUTOEXEC.BAT.)

Multimedia Computer

Most new computers being sold these days are *multimedia computers,* which come equipped with a CD-ROM drive and a sound card. Both of these additions affect the computer's configuration files.

CONFIG.SYS

```
device=c:\dos\himem.sys
device=c:\dos\emm386.exe noems
dos=high
dos=umb
buffers=10
files=30
devicehigh=c:\dev\mtmcdd.sys /d:mscd001 /
p:300 /a:0 /m:16 /t:3 /i:5
shell=c:\dos\command.com c:\dos\ /e:512 /p
```

AUTOEXEC.BAT

```
@echo off
prompt $p$g
path c:\windows;c:\dos;c:\123;c:\util
c:\dos\mscdex.exe /s /d:mscd001 /l:e
c:\dos\smartdrv.exe
set blaster=a220 i2 d1 t4
c:\sbpro\sbp-set /m:12 /voc:12 /cd:12
fm:12
win
```

Notes

The **device=c:\dos\himem.sys** command in the CONFIG.SYS file activates extended memory. The **dos=high** command stuffs part of MS-DOS into the first 64K of extended memory, which is often called the *high memory area* (HMA).

The **device=c:\dos\emm386.exe noems** command in the CONFIG.SYS file activates upper memory. The **dos=umb** command that appears later instructs DOS to allow programs and drivers to be loaded into upper memory.

The **devicehigh=c:\dev\mtmccd.sys** command in the CONFIG.SYS file loads the device driver that enables the CD-ROM drive. This device driver is different for each CD-ROM manufacturer and should be supplied on a diskette with the CD-ROM drive.

The **c:\dos\mscdex.exe** command in the AUTOEXEC.BAT file enables MS-DOS support for the CD-ROM drive. For details on the switches to use for this command, see the documentation that came with your CD-ROM drive.

The **c:\dos\smartdrv.exe** command in the AUTOEXEC.BAT file creates a disk cache using the computer's extended memory. Because this command follows the MSCDEX command, the CD-ROM drive is cached.

The **set blaster** and **c:\sbpro\sbp-set** commands in the AUTOEXEC.BAT file are required to enable MS-DOS support for the sound card. The exact requirements for these lines vary depending on the make and model of your sound card, so check your documentation. Or, better yet, hope that the sound card's setup program added the required commands to the AUTOEXEC.BAT file automatically.

The **win** command in the AUTOEXEC.BAT file starts Windows.

Part IV
Memory Management Command Reference

This part presents detailed reference information for the MS-DOS commands you use to manage memory. In case you find the notation I use to present command syntax confusing, here are a few pointers:

- Stuff you type verbatim is printed in **bold** type.

- Stuff you must replace with your own information — such as a drive letter or a filename — is printed in *italic* type.

- Stuff that is optional is enclosed in [brackets].

- Alternatives from which you must choose are separated from one another by a vertical | bar.

- Everything is in lowercase letters, but you can freely mix UPPER- and lowercase letters however you want.

- The order in which switches and parameters appear usually doesn't matter. Thus, **mem /p /c** and **mem /c /p** accomplish the same thing.

BUFFERS

Tells MS-DOS how many buffers to create for processing disk input and output.

Where you use it

In your CONFIG.SYS file. The location within CONFIG.SYS is not important.

What it looks like

```
buffers=n
```

or

```
buffers=n,m
```

Switch or option	Function
n	The number of buffers to create (1– 99).
m	The number of secondary buffers (1– 8).

What it costs

Each buffer consumes 532 bytes of memory. Figure 1K for every two buffers and you won't be too far off. For example, figure 5K if you allocate ten buffers.

MS-DOS tries to put the buffers into the high memory area (HMA) if **dos=high** is specified and enough room is available in the HMA for all of the buffers.

Examples

```
buffers=10
```

```
buffers=20,10
```

More stuff

If you use a disk caching program such as SmartDrive, use a low number of buffers (such as 10) and omit the secondary buffers option. If you cannot use SmartDrive because your computer has no extended memory, specify a higher number such as 20 or 30.

Take a gander at Chapter 8 of *MORE DOS For Dummies* for the complete **buffers** picture.

DBLSPACE.SYS

Tells DoubleSpace to try to push itself into upper memory.

Upper Memory

A 384K area of memory that follows immediately after the 640K of conventional memory. On a 386 or better computer, upper memory can be used to hold programs that would otherwise consume conventional memory. This leaves more conventional memory available for DOS application programs.

Where you use it

In your CONFIG.SYS file, usually after any other **device** or **devicehigh** commands.

What it looks like

```
device[high]=[drive:][path]dblspace.sys /move
```

Switch or option	*Function*
[*drive*:][*path*]	The drive and directory path for DBLSPACE.SYS (usually C:\DOS).

What it costs

Nothing, really. If your computer uses DoubleSpace, the DoubleSpace driver must be loaded into memory. DBLSPACE.SYS does nothing more than move the DoubleSpace driver from conventional memory to upper memory, if possible.

Example

```
devicehigh=c:\dos\dblspace.sys /move
```

More stuff

If you omit the **device** or **devicehigh** command that loads
DBLSPACE.SYS, then MS-DOS assumes that you meant to include
a **device=c:\dos\dblspace.sys /move** command. Unfortunately,
this command (**device** instead of **devicehigh**) won't move the
DoubleSpace driver into upper memory. So always make
sure that your CONFIG.SYS file contains the line
devicehigh=c:\dos\dblspace.sys /move if you use DoubleSpace.

See Chapters 7 and 24 of *MORE DOS For Dummies* for more
information about DoubleSpace and the DBLSPACE.SYS driver.

For instructions on adding this device driver to your CONFIG.SYS
file, see the procedure "Adding a Device Driver" in Part II of this
book.

See the entry for the DEVICE and DEVICEHIGH commands in this
part for more information about loading this and other device
drivers into memory.

DEVICE

Loads special programs called *device drivers* into conventional
memory. All you have to know is the name of the device driver file
and you're in business.

Device Driver

A special type of program that is loaded into memory when
MS-DOS starts and remains in memory until the computer is
rebooted. Device drivers usually control access to specific
types of hardware devices but may be used for other purposes
as well.

Where you use it

In your CONFIG.SYS file.

What it looks like

```
device=[drive:][path]filename [dd-parameters]
```

Switch or option	Function
[*drive:*][*path*]filename	The drive, path, and filename of the device driver file. For example, **c:\dos\himem.sys**.
dd-parameters	Switches, options, and other paraphernalia required by the driver.

What it costs

The **device** command itself doesn't require any memory. However, the driver that it loads invariably does.

Examples

```
device=c:\dos\himem.sys
```

```
device=c:\dos\emm386.exe ram
```

More stuff

The **device** command always loads device drivers into conventional memory, even if upper memory is available. In contrast, the **devicehigh** command uses upper memory if possible. I usually use **device** only to load the HIMEM.SYS and EMM386.EXE drivers and use **devicehigh** for all other drivers.

See Chapters 7 and 8 of *MORE DOS For Dummies* for more information about the **device** command.

DEVICEHIGH

Loads special programs called *device drivers* into upper memory, if upper memory is available. If not, then it loads device drivers into conventional memory.

Device Driver

A special type of program that is loaded into memory when MS-DOS starts and remains in memory until the computer is rebooted. Device drivers usually control access to specific types of hardware devices but may be used for other purposes as well.

Upper Memory

A 384K area of memory that follows immediately after the 640K of conventional memory. On a 386 or better computer, upper memory can be used to hold programs that would otherwise consume conventional memory. This leaves more conventional memory available for DOS application programs.

Where you use it

In your CONFIG.SYS file.

What it looks like

```
devicehigh=[drive:][path]filename
    [driver-parameters]
```

or

```
devicehigh [/l:region1[,minsize1][;region2
    [,minsize2][/s]] =[drive:][path]
    filename [dd-parameters]
```

Switch or option	*Function*
[*drive:*][*path*]filename	The drive, path, and filename of the device driver file. For example, **c:\dos\himem.sys**.
dd-parameters	Switches, options, and other doodads required by the driver.
/**l**:*region1*[,*minsize1*]	
[;*region2*[,*minsize2*]	(DOS 6.0) Specifies the region or regions of upper memory in which the driver is to be loaded. Omit all of this stuff to avoid becoming a nerd. The *minsize* parameters let you tell DOS to load the driver into the specified region only if the region is as large as the *minsize* value.
/**s**	Used by MemMaker to shrink the UMB while loading the driver. Must be used in conjunction with the /l parameters.

What it costs

The **devicehigh** command itself doesn't require any memory. However, the driver that it loads will require upper or conventional memory.

Examples

```
devicehigh=c:\dos\ansi.sys
```

```
devicehigh=c:\dos\ramdrive.sys 512 /e
```

```
devicehigh=c:\dos\/l:2 c:\dos\mouse.sys
```

More stuff

The **devicehigh** works just like the **device** command, except that it tries to load the device driver into an upper memory block if a large enough block is available. Because **devicehigh** places the driver in conventional memory if there isn't enough upper memory available, I recommend you use **devicehigh** instead of **device** for all your device drivers except HIMEM.SYS and EMM386.EXE.

The following commands should appear in your CONFIG.SYS before (that is, above) any **devicehigh** commands:

```
device=c:\dos\himem.sys
device=c:\dos\emm386.exe ram
dos=umb
```

See Chapters 7 and 8 of *MORE DOS For Dummies* for more information about the **device** command.

DOS=HIGH and DOS=UMB

Tells MS-DOS to load itself into the high memory area and/or to enable support for upper memory blocks (UMBs).

High Memory

The first 64K of extended memory, which can be used almost as if it were extra conventional memory by utilizing an advanced programming technique formally known as "smoke and mirrors." Smoke and mirrors works only on 386 or better computers. The 64K in question is often referred to as the *high memory area*, or *HMA*.

Upper memory

A 384K area of memory that follows immediately after the 640K of conventional memory. On a 386 or better computer, upper memory can be used to hold programs that would otherwise consume conventional memory. This leaves more conventional memory available for DOS application programs.

Where you use it

In your CONFIG.SYS file. The location within CONFIG.SYS is not important.

What it looks like

```
dos=high|low[,umb|,noumb]
```

or

```
dos=[high,|low,]umb|noumb
```

Switch or option	Function
high	Loads portions of MS-DOS into the high memory area (HMA).
low	Does not load MS-DOS into the high memory area (HMA).
umb	Enables support for upper memory blocks (UMBs).
noumb	Does not enable support for upper memory blocks (UMBs).

What it costs

Nothing. In fact, it saves memory.

Examples

```
dos=high
```

```
dos=umb
```

```
dos=high,umb
```

More stuff

You must include a **device=c:\dos\himem.sys** command in the CONFIG.SYS file in order for **dos=high** or **dos=umb** to work.

Although you can include both **high** and **umb** on the same DOS command, I recommend you use separate **dos=high** and **dos=umb** commands instead. That makes it easier to disable one option or the other if the need arises.

Turn to Chapters 8 and 25 of *MORE DOS For Dummies* for additional help with this command.

DRVSPACE

Tells DriveSpace to try to force its way into upper memory.

Upper Memory

A 384K area of memory that follows immediately after the 640K of conventional memory. On a 386 or better computer, upper memory can be used to hold programs that would otherwise consume conventional memory. This leaves more conventional memory available for DOS application programs.

Where you use it

In your CONFIG.SYS file, usually after any other **device** or **devicehigh** commands.

What it looks like

```
device[high]=[drive:][path]drvspace.sys /move
```

Switch or option	Function
[*drive*:][*path*]	The drive and directory path for DRVSPACE.SYS (usually C:\DOS)

What it costs

Zilch. If your computer uses DriveSpace, the DriveSpace driver must be present in memory one way or another. DRVSPACE.SYS does nothing more than move the DriveSpace driver from conventional memory to upper memory if possible.

Example

```
devicehigh=c:\dos\drvspace.sys /move
```

More stuff

If you omit the **device** or **devicehigh** command that loads DRVSPACE.SYS, then MS-DOS assumes that you meant to include a **device=c:\dos\drvspace.sys /move** command. Unfortunately, this command (**device** instead of **devicehigh**) won't move the DriveSpace driver into upper memory. So always make sure that your CONFIG.SYS file contains the line **devicehigh=c:\dos\drvspace.sys /move** if you use DriveSpace.

 See Chapters 7 and 24 of *MORE DOS For Dummies* for more information about DriveSpace and the DRVSPACE.SYS driver.

EMM386 (DOS Command)

Enables or disables expanded memory support provided by the EMM386 device driver.

Where you use it

At the MS-DOS prompt.

What it looks like

```
emm386 [on|off|auto][w=on|w=off]
```

Switch or option	Function
on|off|auto	Activates (**on**) or deactivates (**off**) support for expanded memory, or activates automatic mode (**auto**), in which the EMM386.EXE enables expanded memory support whenever necessary.
w=on|w=off	Activates (**on**) or deactivates (**off**) support for a Weitek coprocessor. If you don't know what this is, you don't have one, so you can ignore this option.

What it costs

Nothing.

Example

```
C:\>emm386 on
```

More stuff

See Chapter 15 in *DOS For Dummies* for instructions on how to use this command.

EMM386.EXE (Device Driver)

Enables support for upper memory and uses extended memory to simulate expanded memory.

Upper Memory

A 384K area of memory that follows immediately after the 640K of conventional memory. On a 386 or better computer, upper memory can be used to hold programs that would otherwise consume conventional memory. This leaves more conventional memory available for DOS application programs.

Extended Memory

Any memory beyond the first 1MB of memory on an 80286 or later computer. If you buy a computer with 4MB of memory, you get 3MB of extended memory. My computer with 20MB of memory has 19MB of extended memory.

Expanded Memory

A special type of memory that was used long ago to provide additional memory for 8088-type computers. True expanded memory resides on a special card that is inserted into one of the computer's expansion slots. However, 386 or better computers can use extended memory to simulate expanded memory. Expanded memory is also known as EMS memory, which stands for something you don't really need to know.

Where you use it

In CONFIG.SYS, following the **device=c:\dos\himem.sys** command.

What it looks like

```
device=[drive:][path]emm386.exe [on|off|auto]
    [memory] [min=size][w=on|w=off]
    [mx|frame=address|/pmmmm] [pn=address]
    [x=mmmm-nnnn][i=mmmm-nnnn] [b=address]
    [l=minxms] [a=altregs] [h=handles] [d=nnn]
    [ram=mmmm-nnnn] [noems] [novcpi]
    [highscan] [verbose] [win=mmmm-nnnn]
    [nohi] [rom=mmmm-nnnn] [nomovexbda]
    [altboot]
```

Switch or option	Function
[*drive*:][*path*]	The drive and directory path for EMM386.EXE (usually C:\DOS).
on|**off**|**auto**	Activates (**on**) or deactivates (**off**) support for expanded memory, or activates automatic mode (**auto**), in which the EMM386.EXE enables expanded memory support whenever necessary.
memory	The amount of expanded memory you want EMM386.EXE to simulate in kilobytes, from 64 through 32,768. Omit it and EMM386.EXE creates as much expanded memory as possible. Any amount you specify is rounded down to the nearest multiple of 16 (the DOS programmer jocks in Redmond love to do stuff like that).
min=*size*	(DOS 6.0) The minimum amount of expanded memory that will be created.
w=on|**w=off**	Activates (**on**) or deactivates (**off**) support for a Weitek coprocessor. If you don't know what this is, you don't have one, so you can ignore this option.

(continued)

Switch or option	Function
mx	The first of three ways to specify the memory address of the EMS page frame. Specify a number from 1– 14 for x, as follows:

1	C000h	8	DC00h
2	C400h	9	E000h
3	C800h	10	8000h
4	CC00h	11	8400h
5	D000h	12	8800h
6	D400h	13	8C00h
7	D800h	14	9000h

Switch or option	Function
frame=*address*	The second of three ways to specify the memory address of the EMS page frame. Specify *address* as the address where you want the page frame to begin. For example, **frame=c800**.
/pmmmm	The third of three ways to specify the memory address of the EMS page frame. Specify *mmm* as the segment number where you want the page frame to begin. For example, **/pc800**.
pn=*address*	Places specific EMS pages at specific memory addresses. Use *n* to specify the page number (0 – 256) and *address* to specify the address of the page. For example, **/p1=c0000h.**
x=*mmmm-nnnn*	Excludes a range of addresses so those addresses won't be used for the EMM page frame or an upper memory block. This option is used when an adapter card uses memory in a way that can't be detected by EMM386.EXE. (Network adapter cards are notorious for this type of behavior.) You can use this option more than once to exclude several ranges.
i=*mmmm-nnnn*	Includes a range of addresses even if it appears that those memory locations are used by an adapter card. If you specify the same range (or an overlap-

ping range) in both an **i** option and an
x option, then the **x** option wins; the
overlapping addresses are excluded.
You can use this option more than
once to include several ranges.

b=*address*   The lowest address that may be used
for EMS banking, which has nothing to
do with investments or loans. *Address*
can be in the range of 1000h through
4000h.

l=*minxms*   Leaves *minxms* kilobytes of extended
memory available.

a=*altregs*   The number of alternate register sets
to allow for multitasking. *Altregs* can
range from 0 through 254. The default
is 7, and there's little reason why any
normal person would need to specify
otherwise. Each alternate register set
consumes about 200 bytes of memory.

h=*handles*   The number of EMS handles, which
are little protrusions that DOS
programs can hold on to when using
EMS. The default of 64 is enough for all
but the most frantic programs, so skip
this option unless someone older and
wiser tells you to use it.

d=*nnn*   The amount of memory used for DMA
buffering, from 16 through 256. The
default is 16. Increase this number if
you get weird error messages about
DMA buffer errors.

ram[=*mmmm-nnnn*]   Enables upper memory as well as
expanded memory. This option is
usually used by itself, without an
address range. This causes EMM386 to
use as much upper memory space as it
can find. When used with an address
range (for example, **ram=e000-ec00**),
the **ram** option tells EMM386 to create
an upper memory block (UMB) using a
specific memory range.

(continued)

Switch or option	Function
noems	Creates upper memory blocks but does not provide support for expanded memory (EMS). Because fewer and fewer programs rely on EMS memory, but most DOS programs can benefit from the increased conventional memory made available when upper memory is used, the **noems** option is among the most popular EMM386 options.
novcpi	(DOS 6.0) Disables VCPI support when used in conjunction with the **noems** option.
highscan	(DOS 6.0) Causes EMM386 to use its high beams when searching for nooks and crannies in upper memory. **Highscan** can often create additional upper memory, but once in awhile it pokes its head in where it doesn't belong and uses memory that should have been left alone. If your computer locks up after using this option, remove it.
verbose	(DOS 6.0) This is the option that, when used along with the EMM386.EXE device driver in your CONFIG.SYS file, causes EMM386 to emit voluminous messages describing in vivid detail its status as it loads itself into memory and activates its various and sundry features, such as expanded memory (often referred to using the initials *EMS*) and upper memory blocks (lovingly known as UMBs), in an effort to keep you informed so that you will at all times and in all places know exactly what the EMM386.EXE device driver is doing, in case you have a deep-seated emotional need to know such things. Omit this option and EMM386 stops yacking.

win=*mmmm-nnnn* (DOS 6.0) Sets aside a specific range of addresses for Windows to use. This option is useful only if you run DOS programs that require as much conventional memory as possible from Windows.

nohi (DOS 6.0) Forces EMM386.EXE to load itself into conventional memory. If you omit this option, EMM386 places a portion of itself in upper memory. This is one of those options best left alone.

rom=*mmmm-nnnn* (DOS 6.0) A finicky option that copies your ROM memory into the specified range of upper memory. This cool technique is called *shadow RAM*, but most newer computers have shadow RAM already built in, so you should skip this option.

nomovexbda (DOS 6.0) EMM386 likes to copy a 1K area of memory called the *extended BIOS data area* from its usual location at the very top of conventional memory into an upper memory block. This option tells EMM386 to keep its greedy little paws off the extended BIOS data area, because every once in awhile some odd-ball program won't work if the data area has been moved. Use this option only if EMM386.EXE seems to be fouling up a program that works fine without EMM386.EXE.

altboot (DOS 6.0) On some computers, EMM386.EXE interferes with the three-finger salute (Ctrl-Alt-Delete). If so, the **altboot** option usually helps.

What it costs

EMM386.EXE giveth back more than it taketh. It uses up about 3K of conventional memory but typically frees up 158K or more of upper memory which can be used to load device drivers and other programs that would otherwise have to be loaded into conventional memory.

Examples

```
device=c:\dos\emm386.exe ram
```

```
device=c:\dos\emm386.exe noems
```

```
device=c:\dos\emm386.exe noems
     x=e000-ec00 highscan
```

More stuff

EMM386.EXE is without a doubt the nerdiest of all MS-DOS commands. It has far more switches and parameters than any sane person would want to deal with, but fortunately only a few of them are important in normal circumstances:

- If you need both expanded memory and upper memory, use the **ram** switch.

- If you want to enable upper memory but you don't need expanded memory, use the **noems** switch.

- If you have a lot of device drivers (for example, if you use a network), try the **highscan** switch. Remove **highscan** if your computer doesn't seem to work right after adding it.

- Wear a hard hat and eye protection when using any of the other options.

See Chapter 15 in *DOS For Dummies* for instructions on how to use this command.

See the entry for the DEVICE command in this part for more information about loading this and other device drivers into memory.

For instructions on adding EMM386.EXE to your CONFIG.SYS file to simulate expanded memory, see the procedure "Simulating Expanded Memory" in Part II of this book.

FCBS

Tells MS-DOS how many *file control blocks* to create. File control blocks are used only by ancient DOS programs, so you don't need to worry about this command unless you still cling unreasonably to that home budgeting program you bought in 1983.

Where you use it

In your CONFIG.SYS file. The location within CONFIG.SYS is not important.

What it looks like

```
fcbs=x
```

Switch or option	*Function*
x	The number of file control blocks to create, up to 255. The default is 4.

What it costs

Each file control block consumes a whopping 60 bytes of conventional memory.

Example

```
fcbs=8
```

More stuff

Best to ignore this one unless you have a crotchety old program that insists on using file control blocks.

Turn to Chapter 8 of *MORE DOS For Dummies* for more reasons to ignore the FCBS command.

Left to its own, MS-DOS won't let you open more than eight files at a time. In the days when WordStar and VisiCalc ruled the software world, eight files were more than enough. Nowadays, that's not even close, so the FILES command must usually be included in CONFIG.SYS to increase this pathetic limit.

Where you use it

In your CONFIG.SYS file. The location within CONFIG.SYS is not important.

What it looks like

```
files=x
```

Switch or option	Function
x	The number of files that can be open simultaneously. The default is 8. A better choice for most users is 30.

What it costs

Each file creates a doohickey called a *file handle*, which takes a 60-byte bite out of conventional memory. Since the default of eight files requires 480 bytes, specifying **files=30** increases the MS-DOS conventional memory requirement by 1,320 bytes.

Example

```
files=30
```

More stuff

Most CONFIG.SYS files should have a FILES command. **Files=30** is a good starting point for most users. If you ever see a message that says "Not enough file handles," then increase the FILES setting a bit and try again.

Chapter 8 of *MORE DOS For Dummies* has more information about the FILES command.

HIMEM.SYS

Enables support for extended memory and the high memory area.

Extended Memory

Any memory beyond the first 1MB of memory on an 80286 or
later computer. If you buy a computer with 4MB of memory, you
get 3MB of extended memory. My computer with 20MB of
memory has 19MB of extended memory.

High Memory

The first 64K of extended memory, which can be used almost as
if it were extra conventional memory by utilizing an advanced
programming technique formally known as "smoke and
mirrors." Smoke and mirrors works only on 386 or better
computers. The 64K in question is often referred to as the *high
memory area*, or *HMA*.

Where you use it

In CONFIG.SYS, before any other DEVICE or DEVICEHIGH commands.

What it looks like

```
device=[drive:][path]himem.sys
[/a20control:on|off] [/cpuclock:on|off]
[/eisa] [/hmamin=m] [/int15=xxxx]
[/numhandles=n] [/machine:xxxx]
[/shadowram:on|off] [/testmem:on|off]
[/verbose]
```

Switch or option	*Function*
[*drive:*][*path*]	The drive and directory path for HIMEM.SYS (usually C:\DOS).

(continued)

Switch or option	Function
/a20control:on | **off**	Specifies whether HIMEM.SYS should take control of some thingamabob called the A20 line even if the A20 line is talking on the telephone when HIMEM.SYS starts up. The default is **/a20control:on**, and even the nerdiest of computer geeks has a tough time coming up with a reason you might want to specify **/a20control:off** .
/cpuclock:on | **off**	Used to correct a problem where HIMEM.SYS causes computers with a "Turbo" speed switch to shift into low gear. Don't use this option unless your computer slows down when HIMEM.SYS is used.
/eisa	(DOS 6.0) Informs HIMEM.SYS that you have one of those fancy EISA-bus computers with more than 16MB of memory.
/hmamin=*m*	Refuses to allow any program that requests less than the specified amount of memory (in kilobytes) to move into the high memory area (HMA). Use this switch if you have a program such as a network device driver that tries to bully its way into the HMA and you want to keep the HMA free for another program which can make better use of it.
/int15=*xxxx*	Long ago, programs accessed extended memory using an interface called the *interrupt 15h interface.* This switch tells HIMEM.SYS to set aside a certain amount of memory (specified in kilobytes) for programs that use this outdated interface.
/numhandles=*n*	If you run several programs that use extended memory and you get a nonsensical message about not having enough handles, use this switch to provide up to 128 handles. The default setting is 32.

Switch or option	*Function*
/machine:*xxxx*	Allows certain computers to function properly with HIMEM.SYS. You can specify *xxxx* as a code or a number according to the following table:

Computer	*Code*	*Number*
Acer 1100	acer1100	6
AT&T 6300 Plus	att6300plus	5
Bull Micral 60	bullmicral	16
CSS Labs	css	12
Dell XBIOS	dell	17
HP Vectra	fasthp	14
HP Vectra (A & A+)	hpvectra	4
IBM 7552 Industrial Computer	ibm7552	15
IBM AT	at	1
IBM PC/AT (alternative delay)	at1, at2, or at3	11, 12, or 13
IBM PS/2	ps2	2
Philips	philips	13
Phoenix Cascade BIOS	ptlcascade	3
Thosiba 1600 & 1200XE	toshiba	7
Tulip SX	tulip	9
Wyse 12.5 Mhz 286	wyse	8
Zenith ZBIOS	zenith	10

/shadowram:on | **off**	(DOS 6.0) Specifies whether HIMEM.SYS should try to turn off the BIOS shadow RAM feature. You can also disable shadow RAM using your computer's BIOS setup routine.

(continued)

/testmem:on | off	(DOS 6.2) Specifies whether or not HIMEM.SYS should test your computers memory when loading. This switch works only with MS-DOS 6.2 or later. Specifying **/testmem:off** can make your computer boot faster.
/verbose	Displays status messages as HIMEM.SYS starts. If you omit this option, HIMEM.SYS displays only error messages.

What it costs

HIMEM.SYS occupies about 1K of conventional memory but can provide access to megabytes of extended memory.

Examples

```
device=c:\dos\himem.sys /testmem:off
```

```
device=c:\dos\himem.sys /machine:ps2
```

More stuff

HIMEM.SYS is one of those commands that has lots of switches that usually aren't necessary. The **/machine** switch may be necessary to get your computer to work with HIMEM.SYS, and **/testmem:off** can save you some time whenever you boot your computer, but you should not attempt to use the other switches without expert advice.

Chapter 25 in *MORE DOS For Dummies* has additional information about HIMEM.SYS.

See the entry for the DEVICE command in this part for more information about loading this and other device drivers into memory.

For instructions on adding HIMEM.SYS to your CONFIG.SYS file to enable extended memory, see the procedure "Activating Extended Memory" in Part II of this book.

INCLUDE

Tells DOS to process the configuration commands that are contained in the specified configuration block.

Where you use it

In your CONFIG.SYS file, but only when you use configuration blocks.

What it looks like

```
include=blockname
```

Switch or option	Function
blockname	The name of the configuration block you want processed.

What it costs

By itself, nothing. The commands that are processed from the configuration block may have their own memory requirements, however.

Example

```
include=network
```

More stuff

The most common use for this command is when you have a configuration menu with several options and two or more of the options share a common set of configuration commands. You could simply duplicate the commands in each menu block that requires them, but the INCLUDE command allows you to place the shared commands in their own block. For example,

```
[menu]
menuitem=Normal
menuitem=Weird
menuitem=Bizarre
menudefault=Normal,10
```

```
[Common]
device=c:\dos\himem.sys /testmem:off
device=c:\dos\emm386.exe noems
dos=high
dos=umb
files=30
buffers=10
[Normal]
devicehigh=c:\dos\ansi.sys
[Weird]
include Normal
devicehigh=c:\dos\ramdrive.sys 1025 /e
[Bizarre]
include Weird
devicehigh=c:\dos\driver.sys /d:1 /f:7
[Common]
```

For instructions on using configuration menus, see the Multiple
Configuration procedures in Part II of this book.

INSTALL

Loads memory-resident programs in the CONFIG.SYS file rather
than in AUTOEXEC.BAT.

Where you use it

In your CONFIG.SYS file.

What it looks like

```
install=[drive:][path]filename
     [command-parameters]
```

Switch or option	*Function*
[*drive*:][*path*]*filename*	The location and filename of the memory-resident program to be loaded.

command-parameters	Switches, parameters, and what-not processed by the program being installed.

What it costs

Depends entirely on the program being loaded. Note that IN-STALL always loads programs into conventional memory. To load a program into upper memory, use the LOADHIGH or LH command instead.

Example

```
install=c:\dos\share.exe
```

More stuff

There's not much point in loading programs via CONFIG.SYS instead of AUTOEXEC.BAT, especially since the LOADHIGH or LH command allows you to load the program into upper memory. So I recommend you steer clear of this command.

LOADFIX

Runs a program, ensuring that the program is not loaded into the first 64K of conventional memory. Use this command if you get the message `Packed file corrupt.`

Where you use it

At the command prompt, when you run a program.

What it looks like

```
loadfix [drive:][path]filename
    [program-parameters]
```

Switch or option	Function
[*drive*:][*path*]*filename*	The program to be run.
program-parameters	Command-line parameters required by the program.

What it costs

LOADFIX uses up any free conventional memory below 64K, so its memory cost depends on how much memory below 64K was free.

Examples

```
loadfix weird /flop
```

```
loadfix c:\progs\weird.exe /flop
```

More stuff

The LOADFIX command fixes a bug found in some programs that prevents them from running in the lowest 64K of conventional memory. This bug won't rear its ugly head if the first 64K of memory is filled with MS-DOS and other programs such as device drivers. But if you've activated upper memory, the buggy programs might find themselves unable to run properly without this command.

LOADHIGH (LH)

Loads memory-resident programs into the upper memory area.

Upper Memory

A 384K area of memory that follows immediately after the 640K of conventional memory. On a 386 or better computer, upper memory can be used to hold programs that would otherwise consume conventional memory. This leaves more conventional memory available for DOS application programs.

Where you use it

In your AUTOEXEC.BAT file. Simply add the keyword **lh** at the beginning of any AUTOEXEC.BAT command that starts a memory-resident program.

What it looks like

```
lh [drive:][path]filename [parameters]
```

or

```
lh [l:region1[,minsize1]][;region2
    [,minsize2]...] [/s]][drive:]
    [path]filename [parameters]
```

If you prefer, you can spell out **lh** as **loadhigh**.

Switch or option	*Function*
[*drive:*][*path*]*filename*	The location and filename of the memory-resident program to be loaded.
parameters	Any parameters or switches required by the program to be loaded.
/l:*region1*[,*minsize1*] [;*regionz*[,*minsize1*]	(DOS 6.0) Specifies one or more regions of upper memory into which the program is to be loaded. MemMaker uses this switch to precisely control the memory location of each of your memory-resident programs. Mere mortals shouldn't mess with it.
/s	(DOS 6.0) Used by MemMaker to shrink the UMB while loading the driver. Must be used in conjunction with the /l parameters.

What it costs

Nothing, actually. In fact, it frees up conventional memory by loading programs into upper memory.

Example

```
lh c:\dos\smartdrv.exe 4096 512
```

More stuff

To use the LOADHIGH command, your CONFIG.SYS file must include DEVICE commands for HIMEM.SYS and EMM386.EXE with the RAM or NOEMS switch, plus you must activate upper memory blocks by including a **dos=umb** command.

LOADHIGH can be used with the following MS-DOS commands:

APPEND	KEYBD	PRINT	GRAPHICS
DOSKEY	MODE	SHARE	NLSFUNC

Chapter 25 of *MORE DOS For Dummies* has more information about the FILES command.

MEM

Displays information about your computer's memory, including how conventional, upper, extended, and expanded memory are utilized.

Upper Memory

A 384K area of memory that follows immediately after the 640K of conventional memory. On a 386 or better computer, upper memory can be used to hold programs that would otherwise consume conventional memory. This leaves more conventional memory available for DOS application programs.

Extended Memory

Any memory beyond the first 1MB of memory on an 80286 or later computer. If you buy a computer with 4MB of memory, you get 3MB of extended memory. My computer with 20MB of memory has 19MB of extended memory.

Expanded Memory

A special type of memory that was used long ago to provide additional memory for 8088-type computers. True expanded memory resides on a special card that is inserted into one of the computer's expansion slots. However, 386 or better computers can use extended memory to simulate expanded memory. Expanded memory is also known as EMS memory, which stands for something you don't really need to know.

Where you use it

At the MS-DOS prompt.

What it looks like

For MS-DOS 6.0 and later:

```
mem [/c|/d|/f|/module modulename] [/p]
```

For MS-DOS 5.0 and earlier:

```
mem [/c|/d|/p]
```

Switch or option	*Function*
/c	Displays a list of programs that are currently loaded into memory, showing how much conventional and upper memory is used by each. If you like to type, you can spell out the word **/classify**.
/d	Displays a list of programs and internal drivers, showing the segment address, size, and module type of each. Normal users find this display impressive but not very useful. The long form of the **/d** switch is **/debug**.
/f	(DOS 6.0) Lists the free areas of conventional and upper memory. This is the switch to use if you want to futz with the LOADHIGH and DEVICEHIGH

(continued)

Switch or option	Function
	commands to load programs into specific upper memory locations. The long form of **/f** is **/free**.
/m *modulename*	(DOS 6.0) Displays detailed information about a specific program module. For example, type **mem /m:doskey** to find out how much memory the DOSKEY command is using.
/p	For MS-DOS 6.0 and later, **/p** pauses the display after each screenful of information and can be spelled out **/page**.
	For MS-DOS 5.0 and earlier, **/p** displays the status of programs loaded into memory and can be spelled out **/program**.

What it costs

Not a penny.

Examples

```
C:\DOS>mem
```

```
C:\DOS>mem /c /p
```

```
C:\DOS>mem /m:doskey
```

More stuff

You'll use this command a lot as you tinker with memory configuration, so get used to it.

You can find more information about the MEM command in Chapter 25 of *MORE DOS For Dummies*.

MEMMAKER

 Automatically configures your computer's memory so you can
pretty much ignore everything else in this book. Well, that's the
idea, anyway. It does its level best to stuff as many programs into
upper memory as can possibly fit.

Upper Memory

A 384K area of memory that follows immediately after the 640K
of conventional memory. On a 386 or better computer, upper
memory can be used to hold programs that would otherwise
consume conventional memory. This leaves more conventional
memory available for DOS application programs.

Where you use it

At the MS-DOS prompt. Exit from Windows if Windows is running,
and don't use this command when you're in a hurry; it takes a few
minutes and demands your full attention.

What it looks like

```
memmaker [/b] [/batch] [/session]
     [/swap:drive] [/t] [/undo] [/w:n,m]
```

Switch or option	Function
/b	Switches to black-and-white mode, which is useful on some types of monochrome monitors.
/batch	Runs MemMaker in automatic mode, without asking questions. If something goes wrong, MemMaker restores your previous versions of CONFIG.SYS, AUTOEXEC.BAT, and SYSTEM.INI (if necessary). When MemMaker finishes, you can review what it did by editing the MEMMAKER.STS file.

(continued)

Switch or option	*Function*
/session	This switch is used by MemMaker when it reboots your computer and should never be used by a low-end user such as yourself. If you do use this switch, Bill Gates will personally come to your office and drag his fingernails across the nearest chalkboard.
/swap:*drive*	If you use older disk compression software that swaps drive letters after your computer starts up, use this switch to tell MemMaker the drive letter that is currently assigned to your boot drive. (This switch is not necessary with DoubleSpace, DriveSpace, Stacker 2.0 or later, and SuperStore.)
/t	Directs MemMaker to ignore IBM Token-Ring networks. Use this switch only if the network is causing MemMaker to run amok.
/undo	This is the Oops! switch, which tells MemMaker that you liked things better the way they were, and please put my computer back together, thank you.
/w:*n,m*	Specifies the amount of upper memory to reserve for those pesky Windows translation buffers, which have nothing to do with NAFTA or GATT.

What it costs

Silly question! MemMaker *saves* you memory!

Examples

```
C:\DOS>memmaker
```

```
C:\DOS>memmaker /batch
```

More stuff

The best way to use MemMaker is without any parameters. Just follow the instructions that appear on-screen. You'll have to tell MemMaker whether or not you want it to create expanded memory, and you have to press Enter a few times, but otherwise you get to sit back and watch MemMaker automatically perform the painstaking task of configuring your memory as efficiently as possible.

Turn to Chapter 25 of *MORE DOS For Dummies* for additional information about MemMaker.

A step-by-step procedure for using MemMaker is found at "Optimizing Memory with MemMaker" in Part II of this book.

MENUCOLOR (CONFIG.SYS)

Changes the color of an MS-DOS 6.0 configuration menu.

Where you use it

In your CONFIG.SYS file, within the [menu] block.

What it looks like

```
menucolor=x[,y]
```

Switch or option	*Function*
x	The text color.
y	The background color.

x and *y* may be any of the following:

Number	*Color*	*Number*	*Color*
0	Black	8	Gray
1	Blue	9	Bright blue
2	Green	10	Bright green
3	Cyan	11	Bright cyan

(continued)

Number	Color	Number	Color
4	Red	12	Bright red
5	Magenta	13	Bright magenta
6	Brown	14	Yellow
7	White	15	Bright white

What it costs

As Bert said to the Constable in *Mary Poppins*, "No charge."

Example

```
menucolor 15,1
```

More stuff

Setting the menu color is a nice idea if you are forced at gunpoint to create configuration menus, but a better idea is to not mess with the menus at all, if you can avoid it.

For instructions on using configuration menus, see the Multiple Configuration procedures in Part II of this book.

MENUDEFAULT

Sets the default menu choice if the user doesn't pick an option within a specified time.

Where you use it

In your CONFIG.SYS file, within the [menu] block.

What it looks like

```
menudefault=blockname[,timeout]
```

Switch or option	Function
blockname	The name of the block that is chosen by default if you sit staring at the configuration menu screen for too long.
timeout	How long (in seconds) the user can stare at the configuration menu screen before the default is taken.

What it costs

Zilch.

Example

```
menudefault Normal,10
```

More stuff

Using the MENUDEFAULT command ensures that you won't turn on your computer, go to fetch a cup of coffee, and then return ten minutes later to find your computer still waiting for you to pick a configuration option. I highly recommend it, if you are among the unfortunate who must use a configuration menu at all.

For instructions on using configuration menus, see the Multiple Configuration procedures in Part II of this book.

MENUITEM

Creates a configuration menu option.

Where you use it

In your CONFIG.SYS file, within a menu block.

What it looks like

```
menuitem=blockname[,text]
```

Switch or option	*Function*
blockname	The name of the block that contains the commands that are processed if you pick this option. The block name can be up to 70 characters in length but cannot contain spaces or the following characters: \ / , ; = [ ]
text	The text that is displayed for this option in the configuration menu. Menu text can be up to 70 characters in length and can contain any combination of letters, numbers, special characters, and spaces. If you omit *text*, *blockname* is displayed instead.

What it costs

This one is a freebie.

Example

```
[menu]
menuitem Normal,Normal Configuration
menuitem Nonet,Normal Configuration, No
    Network
menuitem Games,DOS Games
```

More stuff

Use one MENUITEM command for each option that you want to appear on a configuration menu. The options you want to appear on the main configuration menu should appear within the [menu] configuration block. To create a submenu, use a SUBMENU command in the [menu] block; then use MENUITEM commands in the submenu block.

The CONFIG environment variable is set to the block name corresponding to the menu option chosen by the user. You can test this variable in your AUTOEXEC.BAT file to further customize your configuration; for example, to set a different PATH depending on the configuration selected.

For instructions on using configuration menus, see the Multiple Configuration procedures in Part II of this book.

MSD

Displays information about your computer, including its memory. Alternatively, MSD can write a detailed configuration report to a file.

Where you use it

On your favorite Chinese dish or at the MS-DOS prompt.

What it looks like

```
msd [/b] [/i]
```

or

```
msd [/i] [/f[drive:][path]filename]
     [/p[drive:][path]filename]
     [/s[drive:][path]filename]
```

Switch or option	Function
/b	Runs MSD in black and white.
/i	Bypasses MSD's initial hardware tests, which sometimes cause MSD to stall.
/f[drive:][path]filename	Creates a complete report in the specified file after first prompting you to enter your name, company, address, country, phone number, and comments.
/p[drive:][path]filename	Creates a complete report in the specified file without prompting you for information.
/s[drive:][path]filename	Creates a summary report in the specified file without prompting you for information.

What it costs

Not a penny.

Examples

```
C:\DOS>msd
```

```
C:\DOS>msd /f:msd.txt
```

More stuff

The main reason Microsoft includes the MSD command is so that you can create an MSD report and send it to them in the event you require technical help. The MSD report contains just about every bit of trivia that can be extracted from your computer which might be useful in troubleshooting. Most of what's in the MSD report may look like complete gibberish to you, but to a certified Computer Nerd, it's a goldmine of information. Hand a computer nerd an MSD report and a bag of Cheetos and she'll gladly solve any technical problems you might have.

Chapter 25 of *MORE DOS For Dummies* discusses the MSD command.

RAMDRIVE.SYS

Creates a RAM drive using extended or expanded memory.

RAM Drive

A simulated disk drive that uses extended or expanded memory instead of actual disk storage. Because RAM memory is much faster than disk storage, data can be read to and written to a RAM drive much faster than a real disk drive. However, any data in a RAM drive is permanently lost when you turn your computer off or reboot it. As a result, critical information such as data files should not be stored on a RAM drive.

Extended Memory

Any memory beyond the first 1MB of memory on an 80286 or later computer. If you buy a computer with 4MB of memory, you get 3MB of extended memory. My computer with 20MB of memory has 19MB of extended memory.

Expanded Memory

A special type of memory that was used long ago to provide additional memory for 8088-type computers. True expanded memory resides on a special card that is inserted into one of the computer's expansion slots. However, 386 or better computers can use extended memory to simulate expanded memory. Expanded memory is also known as EMS memory, which stands for something you don't really need to know.

Where you use it

In your CONFIG.SYS file, after the DEVICE commands that load HIMEM.SYS and EMM386.EXE.

What it looks like

```
device[high]=[drive:][path]ramdrive.sys
[disksize [sectorsize [numentries]]] [/e|/a]
```

Switch or option	*Function*
[*drive*:][*path*]	The drive and path location of RAMDRIVE.SYS (usually, C:\DOS).
disksize	The size of the RAM disk to create, in kilobytes. The size can be from 4 to 32,767; and the default is 64. Obviously, you cannot specify an amount that is larger than the amount of memory available.
sectorsize	The sector size for the RAM disk. You can specify 128, 256, or 512, but you should use the default of 512 unless you receive a personal call from Bill Gates directing you to do otherwise.

Switch or option	Function
numentries	The number of files and directories you can create in the root directory of the RAM drive. You can specify from 2 to 1,024; the default is 64. Each directory entry requires 32 bytes, which is why the default is so low. If you need to put more than 64 files in a RAM disk, it's better to create a subdirectory to hold the files rather than increase the size of the number of root directory entries.
/e	Directs RAMDRIVE.SYS to use extended memory for the RAM drive.
/a	Directs RAMDRIVE.SYS to use expanded memory for the RAM drive.
	If you omit both /e and /a, then the RAM drive is created in conventional memory.

What it costs

About 1K, plus the memory required for the disk itself as specified in the *disksize* parameter.

Example

```
devicehigh=c:\dos\ramdrive.sys 512 /e
```

More stuff

Never forget that the contents of a RAM drive are lost whenever you restart or turn off your computer. Never use it to hold important data files! Instead, use it for temporary files or programs that you frequently run.

The general-purpose disk cache created by the SMARTDRV command is usually a more efficient use of extended memory. I recommend you use it instead of RAMDRIVE.SYS.

Chapter 24 of *MORE DOS For Dummies* tells you everything you could possibly want to know about RAMDRIVE.SYS.

See the entry for the DEVICE and DEVICEHIGH commands in this part for more information about loading this and other device drivers into memory.

Also see the "RAM Drive" procedures in Part II of this book for detailed procedures concerning the use and abuse of RAM drives.

REM

Lets you include helpful comments in your CONFIG.SYS or AUTOEXEC.BAT file.

Where you use it

In your CONFIG.SYS or AUTOEXEC.BAT file, on any line you want MS-DOS to ignore.

What it looks like

```
rem comment to be ignored
```

In CONFIG.SYS, you can use a semicolon instead of the word REM:

```
;comment to be ignored
```

What it costs

Nothing.

Examples

```
rem Last updated 12/15/94.
```

```
;devicehigh=c:\dos\ansi.sys
```

More stuff

 Using REM is a great way to temporarily disable CONFIG.SYS or AUTOEXEC.BAT commands without actually removing them from the file. If you later decide to reinstate the command, all you have to do is remove the word REM.

 Chapter 8 of *MORE DOS For Dummies* suggests other uses for the REM command.

SHELL

Tells MS-DOS where to find the all-important COMMAND.COM file. It can also be used to specify a command processor other than COMMAND.COM.

Where you use it

In your CONFIG.SYS file. The location within CONFIG.SYS is not important.

What it looks like

```
shell=[drive:][path]command.com [device]
[/e:nnnn] [/p] [/msg]
```

Switch or option	Function
[*drive:*][*path*]	The drive and path location for COMMAND.COM, usually C:\DOS.
device	An alternative device to use instead of the keyboard and monitor for input and output. *Device* can be **prn**, **lpt1**, **lpt2**, **lpt3**, **con**, **aux**, **com1**, **com2**, **com3**, or **com4**. If you ever find a reason to use this parameter, let me know.
/e:*nnnn*	Specifies the size of the MS-DOS environment, which is where environment variables including PATH and PROMPT are kept. The default is 256, but that's not big enough. I usually add **/e:512** to the SHELL command in my CONFIG.SYS file.
/p	This switch should always be used on the SHELL statement in CONFIG.SYS.
/msg	Stores messages in memory rather than on disk. This makes MS-DOS run faster, but it consumes more memory. It is usually used only when booting from a floppy disk.

Note: The switches described above are not a part of the SHELL command, but rather belong to COMMAND.COM. If you use a different command processor, its switches may be different.

What it costs

SHELL itself doesn't require any memory, but COMMAND.COM does: about 5K with default settings. If high memory is active, about half of COMMAND.COM is moved into the HMA.

Example

```
shell=c:\dos\command.com /e:512 /p
```

More stuff

This command is added to your CONFIG.SYS file automatically when you run MS-DOS SETUP. However, you may want to increase the environment size (/e).

 Chapter 8 of *MORE DOS For Dummies* has more information about the FILES command.

SMARTDRV

 Creates a disk cache in extended memory to speed up disk access.

Disk cache

An area of extended or expanded memory that is used to hold data that would otherwise have to be read from or written to a disk drive. Because extended or expanded memory is much faster than disk storage, using a disk cache can make your computer run significantly faster. *Cache* is pronounced like *Cash*, which should be a $400 *Jeopardy* answer.

Extended Memory

Any memory beyond the first 1MB of memory on an 80286 or later computer. If you buy a computer with 4MB of memory, you get 3MB of extended memory. My computer with 20MB of memory has 19MB of extended memory.

Where you use it

In your AUTOEXEC.BAT file. For MS-DOS 6.2 and later, place it after the MSCDEX command if you have a CD-ROM drive.

What it looks like

```
smartdrv [/x] [[drive[+|-]]...] [/u] [/c|/r]
[/f|/n] [/l] [/v|/q|/s] [initcachesize
[wincachesize]] [/e:elementsize]
[/b:buffersize]
```

Switch or option	Function
/x	(MS-DOS 6.2 and later.) Disables write caching for all drives. (Read caching is still enabled.)
drive[+|-]...	Specifies which drives are to be cached and how. To enable read but not write caching for a drive, specify the drive letter and nothing else. To enable read and write caching for a drive, specify the drive letter followed by a plus sign. To disable all caching for a drive, specify the drive letter followed by a minus sign.
	If you don't specify any drive letters, SMARTDRV read caches floppy drives and read/write caches hard drives.
/u	(MS-DOS 6.2 and later.) Does not load the portion of SMARTDRV that caches CD-ROM drives.
/c	Forces MS-DOS to write cached data to disk.

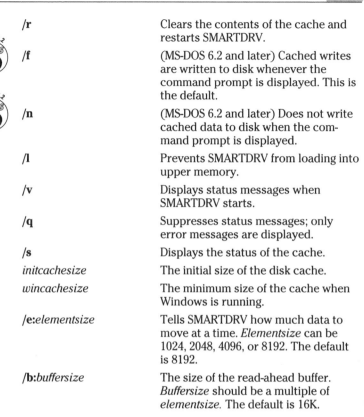

/r	Clears the contents of the cache and restarts SMARTDRV.
/f	(MS-DOS 6.2 and later) Cached writes are written to disk whenever the command prompt is displayed. This is the default.
/n	(MS-DOS 6.2 and later) Does not write cached data to disk when the command prompt is displayed.
/l	Prevents SMARTDRV from loading into upper memory.
/v	Displays status messages when SMARTDRV starts.
/q	Suppresses status messages; only error messages are displayed.
/s	Displays the status of the cache.
initcachesize	The initial size of the disk cache.
wincachesize	The minimum size of the cache when Windows is running.
/e:*elementsize*	Tells SMARTDRV how much data to move at a time. *Elementsize* can be 1024, 2048, 4096, or 8192. The default is 8192.
/b:*buffersize*	The size of the read-ahead buffer. *Buffersize* should be a multiple of *elementsize*. The default is 16K.

The default sizes for *initcachesize* and *wincachesize* depend on the amount of extended memory available on your computer, as follows:

Extended Memory	*Initcachesize*	*Wincachesize*
Up to 1MB	All extended memory	Zero (no caching)
Up to 2MB	1MB	256K
Up to 4MB	1MB	512K
Up to 6MB	2MB	1MB
Over 6MB	2MB	2MB

What it costs

Aside from the extended memory that is used for the cache itself, SMARTDRV uses about 30K of conventional or upper memory with default settings.

Examples

```
c:\dos\smartdrv
```

```
c:\dos\smartdrv /x
```

```
c:\dos\smartdrv c+ d-
```

More stuff

Using the SMARTDRV command is one of the best ways to improve your computer's overall performance. SMARTDRV's default settings for the initial cache size and the Windows cache size are usually adequate, so you don't need to mess with those parameters. Just make sure your AUTOEXEC.BAT file contains a SMARTDRV command.

Beginning with MS-DOS 6.2, SMARTDRV can cache CD-ROM drives as well as floppy and hard disks. To make sure your CD-ROM drive is cached, place the SMARTDRV command after the MSCDEX command in AUTOEXEC.BAT.

If you use 32-Bit File Access in Windows for Workgroups 3.11, then SMARTDRV isn't used to cache hard drives while Windows is running. Instead, Windows for Workgroups uses its own, more efficient 32-bit file cache called VCACHE. In this case, you may want to direct SMARTDRV to cache only floppy drives:

```
c:\dos\smartdrv a b
```

SMARTDRV's write caching is one of the more controversial features of MS-DOS. Because write caching holds data intended for the disk drive in cache memory, often for several seconds, it's possible that a power failure at an inopportune moment can cause lost data. The risk is small, though, and Microsoft enhanced SMARTDRV for MS-DOS 6.2 so that cached data is written to disk more frequently.

The main point to remember when using SMARTDRV with write caching is never to turn off your computer without first exiting from Windows. (If Windows crashes or a power failure occurs while Windows is running, use the SCANDISK command when your computer starts back up to correct any disk errors that may have occurred.)

In earlier versions of MS-DOS (prior to 5.0), SmartDrive was a device driver loaded in CONFIG.SYS rather than a command run from AUTOEXEC.BAT. If you have a **device=c:\dos\smartdrv.sys** command in your CONFIG.SYS file, remove it before adding a SMARTDRV command to your AUTOEXEC.BAT.

MS-DOS 6.0 also includes a SMARTDRV.EXE device driver that should be loaded in CONFIG.SYS if you have certain types of disk drives. This device driver is discussed in the next section.

You can find an interesting and illuminating discussion of SmartDrive in Chapter 23 of *MORE DOS For Dummies*.

The procedure "Activating SmartDrive" in Part II of this book shows you step-by-step how to add SMARTDRV to your AUTOEXEC.BAT file.

SMARTDRV.EXE

Corrects a compatibility problem that occurs with certain types of disk drives that don't get along with EMM386.EXE or Windows.

Where you use it

In your CONFIG.SYS file.

What it looks like

```
device=[drive:][path]smartdrv.exe
/double_buffer
```

Switch or option	*Function*
[*drive*:][*path*]	The drive and directory location of SMARTDRV.EXE, usually C:\DOS.
/double_buffer	Tells SMARTDRV to provide double buffering for drives that don't get along with EMM386.EXE or Windows.

What it costs

About 2K of conventional memory.

Example

```
device=c:\dos\smartdrv.exe /double_buffer
```

More stuff

When you install MS-DOS 6, the SETUP program tries to determine whether or not you need double-buffering. If so, it automatically adds the SMARTDRV.EXE line to your CONFIG.SYS file.

SMARTDRV.SYS

Creates a disk cache in extended or expanded memory to speed up disk access. SMARTDRV.SYS was replaced by SMARTDRV.EXE in Windows 3.1 and MS-DOS 6. Use SMARTDRV.SYS only if you do not have Windows 3.1 or MS-DOS 6.

Disk Cache

An area of extended or expanded memory that is used to hold data that would otherwise have to be read from or written to a disk drive. Because extended or expanded memory is much faster than disk storage, using a disk cache can make your computer run significantly faster. *Cache* is pronounced like *Cash*, which should be a $400 *Jeopardy* answer.

Extended Memory

Any memory beyond the first 1MB of memory on an 80286 or later computer. If you buy a computer with 4MB of memory, you get 3MB of extended memory. My computer with 20MB of memory has 19MB of extended memory.

Expanded Memory

A special type of memory that was used long ago to provide additional memory for 8088-type computers. True expanded memory resides on a special card that is inserted into one of the computer's expansion slots. However, 386 or better computers can use extended memory to simulate expanded memory. Expanded memory is also known as EMS memory, which stands for something you don't really need to know.

Where you use it

In your CONFIG.SYS file.

What it looks like

```
device=[drive:][path]smartdrv.sys
[initcachesize][wincachesize] [/a]
```

Switch or option	*Function*
[*drive:*][*path*]	The drive and directory location of SMARTDRV.EXE, usually C:\DOS.
initcachesize	The initial size of the disk cache.
wincachesize	The minimum size of the cache when Windows is running.
/a	Directs SMARTDRV to use expanded memory for the disk cache. If you omit **/a**, SMARTDRV uses extended memory.

What it costs

About 13K, plus the memory required for the cache itself.

Example

```
devicehigh=c:\dos\smartdrv.sys 1025 512
```

More stuff

SMARTDRV.SYS has been made obsolete by SMARTDRV.EXE in Windows 3.1 and MS-DOS 6. If you have Windows 3.1 or MS-DOS 6, you should use SMARTDRV.EXE instead, and make sure you remove the **device=c:\dos\smartdrv.sys** command from your CONFIG.SYS file.

See the entry for the DEVICE and DEVICEHIGH commands in this part for more information about loading this and other device drivers into memory.

STACKS

Tells MS-DOS how much memory to use for data stacks used to handle hardware interrupts.

Where you use it

In your CONFIG.SYS file. The location within CONFIG.SYS is not important.

What it looks like

```
stacks=n,s
```

Switch or option	Function
n	The number of stacks. You can specify 0 or any number from 8 through 64.
s	The size of each stack. You can specify 0 or any number from 32 through 512.

For an IBM PC, PC/XT, or PC Portable, the default is **stacks=0,0**. For all other computers, the default is **stacks=9,128**.

What it costs

Multiply *n* by *s* to determine how much memory is required for the stacks. The default setting of 9,128 (for most computers) requires 1,152 bytes.

Example

```
stacks=18,512
```

More stuff

Don't mess with the STACKS command unless you get an error message that says, "Stack Overflow" or "Exception error 12." If you see such a message, add a STACKS command to increase the number and size of stacks beyond the default of **stacks=9,128**.

Chapter 8 of *MORE DOS for Dummies* discusses the STACKS command.

SUBMENU

Creates an option in a configuration menu that directs the user to a submenu.

Where you use it

In your CONFIG.SYS file, within a menu block.

What it looks like

```
submenu=blockname[,text]
```

Switch or option	Function
blockname	The name of the block that defines the submenu that will be displayed if the user selects this option. The block name can be up to 70 characters in length but cannot contain spaces or the following characters: \ / , ; = [ ]
text	The text that is displayed for this option in the menu. Menu text can be up to 70 characters in length and can

Switch or option	*Function*
	contain any combination of letters, numbers, special characters, and spaces. If you omit *text*, *blockname* is displayed instead.

What it costs

Nada.

Example

```
[menu]
submenu=NetMenu,Network Options
submenu=NoNetMenu,Non-network Options


[NetMenu]
menuitem WinNet,Windows with Network
menuitem DOSNet,DOS Only with Network
menuitem IntNet,Interlnk with Network


[NoNetMenu]
menuitem WinNoNet,Windows without Network
menuitem DOSNoNet,DOS Only without Network
menuitem IntNoNet,Interlnk without Network


[common]
device=c:\dos\himem.sys /testmem:off
device=c:\dos\emm386.exe noems
dos=high
dos=umb
shell=c:\dos\command.com /e:512 /p


[WinNet]
include Net
include WinNoNet


[DOSNet]
include Net
include DOSNoNet
```

```
[IntNet]
include Net
include IntNoNet

[WinNoNet]

[DOSNoNet]
devicehigh=c:\ansi.sys
stacks=9,512

[IntNoNet]
devicehigh=c:\dos\interlnk.exe

[common]
```

More stuff

To create a submenu, use a SUBMENU command in the [menu] block; then use MENUITEM commands in the submenu block.

The CONFIG environment variable is set to the block name corresponding to the menu option chosen by the user. You can test this variable in your AUTOEXEC.BAT file to further customize your configuration; for example, to set a different PATH depending on the configuration selected.

For instructions on using configuration menus, see the Multiple Configuration procedures in Part II of this book.

Part V

Troubleshooting

I hope you never have to turn to this part of the book, but if you do, you'll find help with the most common memory management problems.

Your success at troubleshooting these problems is greatly enhanced if you have an emergency boot disk available. See the procedure "Creating a Panic Disk" in Part II of this book for instructions on how to create such a disk. Don't delay! Act now!

I Get a Weird Error Message When My Computer Boots!

The computer's POST (*Power On Self Test*) program, which runs whenever you turn on your computer, has detected an error. If POST detects an error, you get a message such as

```
ERROR HDD Controller Failure
```

or

```
ERROR Keyboard Failure
```

This message is displayed before you see the message Starting MS-DOS.

This type of error is often caused by a hardware problem that can be resolved simply by checking the cables that connect the component in question. For example, if you get a message that indicates a keyboard failure, try unplugging the keyboard and then plugging it back in. Turning the computer off and then on again may clear up the problem as well, if you're lucky.

Sometimes, the cause of a POST failure lies in the CMOS setup, which stores information about your computer's configuration in a small amount of memory that's kept alive at all times by batteries. If the batteries go bad, this information can be lost or corrupted. Sometimes, the POST error message indicates that the problem is incorrect CMOS data, but sometimes it doesn't. So it always pays to run your computer's CMOS setup program before putting your computer out with the trash. The procedure for running the CMOS setup program varies from one computer to the next, so you should check your owner's manual to find out how.

The following table summarizes the POST error messages that are displayed for computers that use AMI BIOS chips. Error messages for computers that use other types of BIOS chips are similar.

POST error message	*What you can do about it*
8042 Gate — A20 Error	Not much. Take it to a shop.
Address Line Short	Uh oh. Haul it to the repair shop.
C: Drive Error	Hmm. If you're gutsy, open up the box and make sure the cables are properly connected. Also, try running the CMOS setup program to ensure that the correct drive type is defined.
C: Drive Failure	Bad news. The hard drive is probably bad. Let's hope it's still under warranty.
Cache Memory Bad, Do Not Enable Cache!	Ouch. Run CMOS setup and make sure cache is disabled. Then, when you get a chance, take the computer to the shop and get the cache memory replaced.
CH- Timer Error	I hate it when this happens. The motherboard probably needs to be replaced.
CMOS Battery State Low	Replace the battery that powers the CMOS. Don't put it off.
CMOS Checksum Failure	Nuts. The CMOS data is scrambled. Hopefully, you copied it down some-where, perhaps in a text file on your

POST error message	What you can do about it
	emergency disk (you did make an emergency disk, right?). Run the CMOS setup program and restore the proper settings. If it happens again, replace the CMOS battery.
CMOS System Options Not Set	See preceding.
CMOS Display Type Mismatch	The CMOS thinks you have a different type of display than you actually do. Run CMOS setup and set the correct display type.
CMOS Memory Size Mismatch	This can happen if the CMOS memory gets scrambled, but it can also happen the first time you start your computer after installing more memory. Run CMOS setup and set the correct amount of memory.
CMOS Time and Date Not Set	Run CMOS setup and set the time and date. If it happens again, replace the battery.
D: Drive Error	Uh oh. Something is wrong with your D drive. (If you don't *have* a D drive, check your CMOS setup.)
D: Drive Failure	Bummer. Your D: drive has gone south for the winter. Take the computer to a repair shop.
Diskette Boot Failure	This can happen when you boot your computer with an unformatted disk in drive A. Remove the disk and try again.
Display Switch Not Proper	Your computer has an improper display switch. Consult your owner's manual for advice on how to make the switch proper.
DMA Error, DMA #1 Error, DMA #2 Error	It's okay to swear when you take your computer to the shop for a motherboard replacement.
FDD Controller Failure	This could be a bad controller card or a bad cable. Try the cable first (it's cheaper).

(continued)

POST error message	*What you can do about it*
HDD Controller Failure	This too could be a bad controller card or a bad cable. Cables are cheaper than controller cards, so check the cable first.
INTR #1 Error, INTR # 2 Error	Sounds like a new motherboard may be needed. Take the computer to a shop.
Invalid Boot Diskette	Something isn't right with the boot disk. Replace it, or remove it and boot from the hard disk.
Keyboard Locked ...Unlock	Unlock your keyboard.
Keyboard Error	This might indicate that your keyboard is defective. If you have a spare keyboard lying around, try using it instead. If the spare keyboard works, replace the defective keyboard. If it doesn't, take the computer to a repair shop.
KB/Interface Error	This is most likely a problem with the keyboard cable or connector. Try another keyboard to make sure.
No ROM BASIC	Huh? This means that the computer couldn't boot from drive A or C.
Off Board Parity Error	A memory chip on an adapter card is defective. Shut the computer off and start it again. If the error persists, take it to a repair shop.
On Board Parity Error	A memory chip on the motherboard is defective. Shut the computer off and start it again. If the error persists, take it to a repair shop.
Parity Error ????	A memory chip is defective. Shut the computer off and start it again. If the error persists, take it to a repair shop.

My Computer Froze Up!

This is the worst nightmare of any computer user — the computer just freezes up, becoming completely unresponsive, kind of like your spouse when you've forgotten his or her birthday. Nothing happens on the display, you bang away at all the keys on the keyboard, hoping something will happen, but your computer just sits there smugly. Your computer has locked up.

What to do

1. Try pressing Escape. If nothing happens...

2. Try pressing Ctrl-C or Ctrl-Break. If nothing happens...

3. If you're in Windows, try pressing Ctrl-Esc. If nothing happens...

4. Press Ctrl-Alt-Delete to restart your computer. If nothing happens...

5. Press the computer's Reset button.

6. When your computer comes back to life, run the SCANDISK command immediately to clean up any disk mess that was left behind when the computer locked up.

7. Now here's the scary part. Try to make it happen again. Do whatever it was you were doing when the computer locked up and see if the problem repeats. If it does...

8. Reboot your computer, but this time press F5 to bypass your CONFIG.SYS and AUTOEXEC.BAT files. Now try to make the computer lock up again. If you cannot cause it to happen, it's time to suspect that something in your CONFIG.SYS or AUTOEXEC.BAT file is causing the problem, possibly a memory conflict. So...

9. Examine your CONFIG.SYS and AUTOEXEC.BAT files, looking for possible conflicts. Eliminate any command that is in the least bit unusual by typing **rem** to make the command a comment. Then reboot and see whether the problem recurs. Repeat the cycle of eliminating suspect commands and rebooting until you've isolated the command that caused the conflict.

I Can't Run My Favorite DOS Program!

All programs that run under MS-DOS have a minimum memory requirement: If a certain amount of conventional memory is not available, then the program refuses to run. The program may display a helpful error message such as There's not enough memory to run your program, or it may display a less-than-helpful message such as Error B37. Or the program may simply lock up.

What to do

1. From the command prompt, run the MEM command and note the size of the largest executable program. For example, the following MEM command output shows that the largest executable program size is 463K:

```
C:\>mem

Memory Type        Total  =   Used  +   Free
--------------     ------     ------     ------
Conventional        640K       177K      463K
Upper               155K        30K      125K
Reserved            384K       384K        0K
Extended (XMS)   19,301K     2,289K   17,012K
                 -------     ------    -------
Total memory     20,480K     2,879K   17,601K

Total under 1 MB    795K       206K      589K

Largest executable program size       463K (474,448 bytes)
Largest free upper memory block       125K (128,144 bytes)
MS-DOS is resident in the high memory area.

C:\>
```

2. Check your program's documentation to find out how much memory is required to run the program. This information is usually found near the beginning of the manual in a section labelled "Requirements," "Minimum System Configuration," or something similar. For example, my very old copy of Print Shop (which I don't use anymore but its manual happened to be within arm's reach when I wrote this) says that it requires 512K of memory.

3. Compare the number you found in step 1 with the number you found in step 2. If the amount of memory available is larger than the amount of memory required, you probably don't have a memory management problem (you might, though; the memory requirement printed in software manuals isn't always accurate). If the amount of memory available is *less* than the amount of memory required, however, you have a memory management problem.

4. Use the various procedures in Part II to optimize your computer's memory so that as much conventional memory as possible is made available. The easiest way to do this is to run the MemMaker program.

5. If there still is not enough memory available, run the MEM /C /P command and double-check to make sure that the programs you think are supposed to be loaded into upper memory actually are being loaded there, and that there isn't a significant amount of upper memory going unused. If a program refuses to load into upper memory, consult the program's manual. Some programs have technical restrictions that prevent them from loading into upper memory.

6. If you are using EMM386.EXE to simulate expanded memory, ask yourself if this is really necessary. Expanded memory gobbles up 64K of upper memory that could be put to better use. Add the /NOEMS switch to the DEVICE command that loads EMM386.EXE to disable expanded memory.

7. As a last resort, consider setting up a configuration menu that allows you to choose one of two configurations when you start your computer: a normal configuration, which loads all of the programs and device drivers you normally need but doesn't provide enough conventional memory for all of your programs, and a lean configuration that sacrifices a few key programs or device drivers (such as network drivers or a CD-ROM driver and the MSCDEX program) but is able to run even your most memory-intensive programs.

I Got a DoubleGuard Alert!

If you use DoubleSpace with MS-DOS 6.2 or DriveSpace with MS-DOS 6.22, a special program called DoubleGuard constantly monitors the memory area used by DoubleSpace or DriveSpace to make sure that no other unauthorized program is interfering with the DoubleSpace/DriveSpace memory. If DoubleGuard detects an interfering program, it halts your computer and displays an ominous message called a "DoubleGuard Alert."

What to do

1. Write down whatever you were doing when you received the message.

2. Restart your computer.

3. Run the following command:

```
C:\>scandisk /all
```

This command corrects any errors that may have cropped up on your disk drive as a result of the DoubleGuard Alert.

4. Take a deep breath.

5. Try to make it happen again.

6. If you can get the problem to happen again, boot clean by pressing F5 when you see the message Starting MS-DOS. Then reintroduce your device drivers and memory-resident programs one at a time, trying to force the DoubleGuard Alert, until you find the culprit.

7. After you find the culprit, contact the company that wrote the offending software. They may have a new version that doesn't conflict with DoubleSpace or DriveSpace, or they may have recommendations for preventing the DoubleGuard Alert.

I Got a Stack Overflow!

If you see a message that says something about a Stack Overflow, follow this procedure.

What to do

1. If the system has halted, restart it by pressing Ctrl-Alt-Delete.

2. Run the following command:

```
C:\>scandisk /all
```

This command corrects any errors that may have cropped up on your disk drive as a result of the Stack Overflow.

3. Edit your CONFIG.SYS file and double the setting of the STACKS command. For example, if CONFIG.SYS contains the command STACKS=9,256, change it to STACKS=18,256. (You can double either the first or the second number.)

4. Save the CONFIG.SYS file and then reboot your computer. Rerun the program that caused the Stack Overflow message to see if it recurs.

5. If the Stack Overflow message recurs, double the STACKS setting again.

MemMaker Got Stuck!

On occasion, MemMaker runs into a snag that causes it to get
stuck. Such snags usually occur when MemMaker restarts your
computer. MemMaker does this twice: the first time to monitor
your current memory configuration so that it can determine a
more efficient configuration, the second time to test its new
configuration.

What to do

If MemMaker stalls after restarting your computer the first time,
follow these steps:

1. Press Ctrl-Alt-Delete to restart your computer. (If Ctrl-Alt-
   Delete doesn't do the trick, then press the Reset button.)

2. MemMaker automatically restarts itself and displays an
   informative screen.

```
Microsoft MemMaker


Your computer was restarted before MemMaker finished determining
the memory requirements of your device drivers and memory-resident
programs.

    If you restarted your computer because it was not working
    properly, choose "Try Again with conservative settings."

    If MemMaker was interrupted for another reason (for example,
    a power failure), or if you are not sure what happened, choose
    "Try again with the same settings."

    To exit MemMaker and restore your system files, choose "Cancel
    and undo all changes."

    Try again or cancel? Try again with conservative settings



ENTER=Accept Selection    SPACE=Change Selection    F1=Help
```

3. Press Enter to select the "Try again with more conservative
   settings" option. Your computer restarts. Then try to
   optimize your memory configuration more cautiously.

4. Follow the instructions that appear on the screen to
   complete MemMaker's memory optimization. If MemMaker
   completes its optimization successfully, you can skip the
   rest of this procedure.

5. If MemMaker stalls again, select the "Cancel and undo all changes" option, and then press Enter to restore your original CONFIG.SYS and AUTOEXEC.BAT files.

6. Type **memmaker** at the command prompt to run MemMaker again.

7. When MemMaker asks whether you want to use Express or Custom setup, select Custom and press Enter.

8. Follow the instructions on-screen until the Advanced Options screen is displayed.

```
Microsoft MemMaker


                        Advanced Options

Specify which drivers and TSRs to include in optimization?     No
Scan the upper memory area aggressively?                       Yes
Optimize upper memory for use with Windows?                    No
Use monochrome region (B000-B7FF) for running programs?        No
Keep current EMM386 memory exclusions and inclusions?          Yes
Move Extended BIOS Data Area from conventional to upper memory? Yes


To select a different option, press the UP ARROW or DOWN ARROW key.
To accept all the settings and continue, press ENTER.



ENTER=Accept All   SPACEBAR=Change Selection   F1=Help   F3=Exit
```

9. Change the "Scan the upper memory area aggressively" option to No by pressing the down arrow and then the spacebar. Press Enter.

10. Follow the remaining MemMaker instructions to optimize your memory.

If MemMaker stalls when it reboots your computer for the second time, you aren't presented with the option of retrying with more conservative settings. Follow this procedure instead:

1. Press Ctrl-Alt-Delete to restart your computer. (If Ctrl-Alt-Delete doesn't do the trick, then press the Reset button.)

2. MemMaker automatically restarts itself and asks whether you want to continue. Select the "Exit and undo changes" option by pressing the spacebar. Then press Enter to reboot your computer using the original CONFIG.SYS and AUTOEXEC.BAT files.

3. Type **memmaker** at the command prompt to run MemMaker again.

4. When MemMaker asks whether you want to use Express or Custom setup, select Custom and press Enter.

5. Follow the instructions on the screen until the Advanced Options screen is displayed. (If you must know what this screen looks like, refer to step 8 of the preceding procedure.)

6. Change the "Scan the upper memory area aggressively" option to No by pressing the down-arrow key and then the spacebar. Press Enter.

7. Follow the remaining MemMaker instructions to optimize your memory.

MemMaker Made Things Worse!

If you find that your computer won't boot after running MemMaker, or if you wind up with *less* conventional memory available than you had before running MemMaker, or if you decide you just don't like MemMaker and want to get rid of it, follow these steps:

What to do

1. If your computer stalls while processing CONFIG.SYS or AUTOEXEC.BAT, press Ctrl-Alt-Delete to reboot your computer. Then press F5 when the message Starting MS-DOS is displayed.

2. Type the following command at the MS-DOS prompt:

   memmaker /undo

   MemMaker confirms that you want to undo changes.

3. Select the "Restore files now" option by pressing Enter. MemMaker restores your system files.

4. Press Enter to restart your computer using your original configuration files.

```
Microsoft MemMaker

You have specified that you want to undo the changes MemMaker made
to your system files.

When you started MemMaker, it made backup copies of your CONFIG.SYS
and AUTOEXEC.BAT files (and, if necessary, your Windows SYSTEM.INI
file).  MemMaker restores these files by replacing the current files
with the backup copies it made earlier.  If the files have changed
since MemMaker made the backup copies, those changes will be lost
when you restore the original files.

            Restore original system files or exit? Restore files now




ENTER=Accept Selection  SPACEBAR=Change Selection  F1=Help  F3=Exit
```

```
Microsoft MemMaker

MemMaker has finished restoring your original CONFIG.SYS and
AUTOEXEC.BAT files (and, if necessary, your Windows SYSTEM.INI
file).

 • To restart your computer with its original memory
   configuration, remove any disks from your floppy-disk
   drives, and then press ENTER.





ENTER=Continue
```

My Packed File Is Corrupt

Just as too much of a good thing can sometimes be bad, too much
memory optimization can sometimes be bad. Most DOS programs
benefit from your efforts to free up as much conventional
memory as possible, but every now and then you come across a
DOS program that was written with the built-in assumption that
MS-DOS uses up a certain amount of conventional memory. Such
programs assume that they will be loaded at a memory location

that is above the first 64K of conventional memory. In ordinary circumstances, all programs run under MS-DOS are loaded above 64K, so these programs aren't a problem. However, using MemMaker might move so much of MS-DOS into upper memory and the high memory area that DOS programs are loaded into a memory location that is below 64K. If that happens, you might get the following message when running a DOS program:

```
Packed file corrupt
```

Don't ask me why; I haven't a clue. This message makes no sense, but fortunately there is an easy way around it.

What to do

Use the LOADFIX command to run the miscreant program. For example,

```
C:\>loadfix oldprog
```

In this example, a program named OLDPROG is run by the LOADFIX command.

See the description of the LOADFIX command in Part IV of this book.

Parity Error? What's a Parity Error?

Parity is a slick computer trick that helps your computer make sure that its memory is operating correctly. A *parity bit* is an extra bit that is added on to the end of each byte of memory. Whenever data is written to a byte of memory, the computer hardware adds up the individual bits that make up the byte. If the resulting number is even (that is, divisible by two), the parity bit is set to 1; otherwise, it is set to 0. As a result, if all nine bits — the eight bits that make up the byte and the parity bit — are added together, then the resulting number should be odd. If the result is even, a *parity error* has occurred and the byte of data at the memory location is not to be trusted.

Back in the old days when computer memory was measured in pounds and computer memory was so big you could actually see each bit with the naked eye, parity errors were commonplace. On today's computers, they are quite rare.

What to do

If you receive a message about a memory parity error, don't panic. It could be that a low-flying meteor passed overhead and momentarily disrupted your computer's circuitry. However, if the parity error persists, take your computer to a repair shop and have it checked out. You may have a defective memory chip.

By the way, playing with your computer's memory configuration cannot directly cause your memory to develop a parity error. However, you may have a defective byte of memory at an upper memory location that wasn't used until you optimized your memory. In that case, it might appear that your optimization efforts caused the parity error to occur. Just tell yourself that you're good enough, you're smart enough, and that nasty ol' parity error isn't your fault. (If you want to blame it on your parents, that's okay too.)

Windows Says My Swap File Is Corrupt

If you receive the message `The swap file is corrupt` when starting Windows, then you need to recreate the permanent swap file. See Part II for instructions.

I Ran MemMaker, and Now Windows Won't Start In Enhanced Mode!

If your computer has but 2MB of memory and Windows refuses to run in Enhanced mode after running MemMaker, the problem may be that although MemMaker freed up conventional memory, it used up valuable extended memory in the process. Windows requires at least 1024K of free extended memory for it to run in Enhanced mode.

What to do

Type the command **memmaker /undo** at the MS-DOS prompt to back out of the changes made by MemMaker, and Windows should jump back to life.

If you have more than 2MB of memory on your computer, follow these steps to make sure that MemMaker is indeed the source of your Windows woes:

1. Press Ctrl-Alt-Delete to restart your computer.

2. The moment you see the message `Starting MS-DOS`, press F8.

3. When MS-DOS displays `device=c:\dos\himem.sys?[Y,N]`, press Y to load HIMEM.SYS.

4. When MS-DOS displays `device=c:\dos\emm386.exe?[Y,N]`, press N to prevent EMM386.EXE from loading.

5. Press Esc to process the rest of CONFIG.SYS and AUTOEXEC.BAT normally.

6. Now try to start Windows. If Windows starts properly, you can assume that the Windows problem is related to MemMaker. If it does not, you have some other problem that is not related to MemMaker, so you can skip the rest of this procedure.

7. Exit from Windows by choosing File⇨Exit.

8. Type **memmaker** at the command prompt to run MemMaker again.

9. When MemMaker asks whether you want to use Express or Custom setup, select Custom and press Enter.

10. Follow the instructions on-screen until the Advanced Options screen is displayed.

```
Microsoft MemMaker


                         Advanced Options


Specify which drivers and TSRs to include in optimization?        No
Scan the upper memory area aggressively?                          Yes
Optimize upper memory for use with Windows?                       No
Use monochrome region (B000-B7FF) for running programs?           No
Keep current EMM386 memory exclusions and inclusions?             Yes
Move Extended BIOS Data Area from conventional to upper memory?   Yes




To select a different option, press the UP ARROW or DOWN ARROW key.
To accept all the settings and continue, press ENTER.




ENTER=Accept All  SPACEBAR=Change Selection  F1=Help  F3=Exit
```

11. Change the `Scan the upper memory area aggressively` option to No by pressing the down arrow and then the spacebar. Press Enter.

12. Follow the remaining MemMaker instructions to optimize your memory.

13. When MemMaker is finished, run Windows to see whether it works correctly. If it does, skip the rest of this procedure.

14. Now we're getting serious. Exit Windows and type the following command at the MS-DOS prompt:

    edit c:\config.sys

15. Type **X=A000-EFFF** at the end of the line that loads EMM386.EXE. For example,

    ```
    device=c:\dos\emm386.exe ram x=a000-efff
    ```

16. Use the File⇨Save command to save the file, and then use the File⇨Exit command to leave the EDIT command.

17. Press Ctrl-Alt-Delete to reboot your computer.

18. Start Windows once again to see if it works. If it does (and it better!), repeat steps 14–17, using a narrower range of addresses each time. Start by reducing the second number. For example, try **x=a000-dfff**. If that works, try **x=a000-cfff** and then **x=a000-bfff**. When you find a combination that doesn't work, revert to the previous range that worked and then start increasing the first number. For example, if **x=a000-dfff** works but **x=a000-cfff** doesn't, try **x=b000-dfff** and then **x=c000-dfff**. Keep narrowing the range until you get the smallest amount of memory excluded that still allows you to start Windows.

19. You've got to be kidding. This is without doubt the nerdiest troubleshooting procedure in the book. If you get past unlucky step 13, consider offering mass quantities of Doritos and Jolt Cola to your friendly computer guru in an effort to get him or her to fix the problem for you.

Windows Says I'm Out of Memory!

Windows has a bad habit of lying about memory problems. It displays messages like Not enough memory when in fact the problem is that an internal memory area, called the System Resource Heap, has become full. This can happen even when you have multiple megabytes of free memory available, because the System Resource Heap is a fixed size no matter how much memory your computer has. Once it's full, it's full.

Low system resources can cause bizarre symptoms, such as dialog boxes that appear without borders, in weird fonts, or in strange colors. Sometimes, the display goes completely haywire.

What to do

1. Save your work if you can. Use the File⇨Save command to save your work; then use File⇨Close to close your file.

2. Exit from as many application programs as possible. Use Alt-Tab to switch to other programs. Then shut them down by using the File⇨Exit command.

3. If Windows appears to be totally locked up, try pressing Ctrl-Alt-Delete. You'll probably get a message to the effect that "the program you were running is no longer responding, and do you want to terminate it?" Shut the program down and then see whether Windows will let you shut down any other programs that are still running in a more orderly fashion. Pressing Ctrl-Alt-Delete is a last-resort option because you lose any work you weren't able to save. But sometimes you have no alternative.

4. After you shut down all of your programs, exit Windows. After you encounter a resource meltdown, it's likely that some portion of the resource heap has been permanently lost. The only way to restore the heap to full working condition is to shut down Windows and restart it. This gives you a fresh resource heap, ready for you to fill up again.

More stuff

The biggest sources of resource problems are programs that use system resources and don't give them back. Such programs are surprisingly common. For example, Word for Windows 6 has at least one known problem which on occasion causes it to consume resources and not release them.

You can often free up some system resources by following the procedures removing unnecessary TrueType fonts and eliminating wallpaper. See the procedures "Removing TrueType Fonts to Conserve Memory" and "Removing Wallpaper to Conserve Memory" in Part II of this book for details.

Part VI

Adding Memory

This part summarizes the options for adding memory to 8088, 80286, and 386 or better systems, as well as the procedures for adding memory chips to your computer.

Memory Expansion Options for 8088 Systems

If you have an aging 8088-based computer such as an IBM PC or PC/XT, then the best advice that I can offer is to leave it overnight in the parking lot of the corner convenience store with the keys in the ignition and hope someone steals it. Short of that, try these ideas:

- Make sure that as much memory as possible is installed on the motherboard. Some 8088 motherboards can accommodate 640K of conventional memory. Others can accommodate only 512K or even 256K. Consult your owners manual (I hope you can find it!), which may ask you to open the case and examine the motherboard to see how much memory is installed.

  Motherboard memory on an 8088 computer usually comes in the form of DIP chips, which must be installed carefully to avoid bending the pins. See the procedure "Installing Motherboard Memory" later in this part.

  After you install the DIP chips, you may have to change a switch or jumper block setting to tell the computer about the new memory you've installed. Unfortunately, the necessary switch or jumper block setting isn't indicated on the motherboard itself, so you need to consult the owner's manual.

- After the motherboard is filled, the only way to expand the capacity of an 8088 computer is to install an expanded memory card. An expansion card with 2MB of memory probably costs about $150. There's not much demand for these cards, so your local computer shop will probably have to special-order it. Or you can order the card yourself from a mail order supplier, if you're in an adventurous mood.

  You may have to install the memory on the expansion card before you actually install the card itself. If the expansion card is new, then it probably accepts SIMM modules. If it is old, then you have to install DIP chips.

Memory Expansion Options for 286 Systems

If you have an 80286 system such as an IBM PC/AT, you can add extended memory to the motherboard, or you can add extended or expanded memory on an expansion card. Which type of memory is better depends on the type of software that you use. If you use a spreadsheet program or other type of program that requires expanded memory, then you're better off adding a separate memory card which can support expanded memory. Otherwise, add extended memory directly to the motherboard.

DIP

Dual Inline Package, a fancy term for "chip." Specifically, a DIP chip is a chip that has a row of pins protruding out and downward along two sides, making the chip look like something you would try to capture in a Roach Motel.

- You can add conventional and extended memory directly to the motherboard in DIP chips. Most of these computers have sockets for at least 1MB of memory; some have sockets for up to 8MB or more of memory installed directly on the motherboard.

  Consult your owner's manual for instructions on how to add memory chips to the motherboard sockets; the owner's manual may contain restrictions about how many chips you can add to each bank of sockets — kind of like the rules for building houses and hotels in Monopoly. When you're ready to add the chips, turn to the procedure "Installing Motherboard Memory" later in this part for help.

After you've installed memory on an 80286 computer, you must run the computer's setup program to tell the computer about the new memory. On 80286 computers, the setup program is usually a separate program that you must run from a disk. Be sure to keep a copy of the setup program in a safe place; if you lose it, you won't be able to reconfigure the computer.

- After the motherboard memory sockets are filled up, the only way to add memory is by adding a memory expansion card. On an 80286 computer, the memory expansion card can be configured for extended memory, expanded memory, or a combination of both. Expansion cards for PC/AT computers are available at a reasonable cost, although your local computer shop may have to special-order it for you. Expansion cards with 2MB of memory installed start at about $150, although the price of memory varies daily like the price of pork bellies.

If you purchase a new memory expansion card, the card probably accepts memory in the form of 1MB or 4MB SIMM modules. If you have an older card, the memory is in the form of DIP chips.

Memory Expansion Options for 386 or Better Systems

Here are the options for adding memory to a computer that uses an 80386, 486, or Pentium processor:

- Always fill the motherboard memory sockets on a 386 or better computer before resorting to an expansion card. Why? Because expansion card memory is always accessed at the speed of the ISA bus, whereas motherboard memory is accessed at the clock speed of the processor. Using a memory expansion board on a 386 or better computer can make the computer crawl at an 80286 pace.

SIMM

Single Inline Memory Module. An effective way of packing
memory in which groups of nine chips are assembled onto a
little card that looks like a mustache comb. SIMMs are readily
available in 1MB and 4MB sizes.

- Newer motherboards accept memory in several banks of
  SIMMs. Check the owner's manual to find out if there are
  restrictions on how you can add SIMM modules. On some
  computers, you have to add SIMM modules four at a time
  and you cannot mix and match. For example, the
  motherboard on my computer has two banks of four SIMM
  sockets and can only be configured in one of the following
  ways:

Bank 1	*Bank 2*	*Total Memory*
Four 256K SIMMs	Empty	1MB
Four 256K SIMMs	Four 256K SIMMs	2MB
Four 1MB SIMMs	Empty	4MB
Four 256K SIMMs	Four 1MB SIMMs	5MB

Bank 1	*Bank 2*	*Total Memory*
Four 1MB SIMMs	Four 1MB SIMMs	8MB
Four 4MB SIMMs	Empty	16MB
Four 4MB SIMMs	Four 1MB SIMMs	20MB
Four 4MB SIMMs	Four 4MB SIMMs	32MB

As you can see, there is no way to configure this computer
with 12MB of memory. Also, if you already have both banks
filled with 1MB SIMMs, the only way to increase the
memory is to replace one or both banks of 1MB SIMMs with
4MB SIMMs.

When you purchase a computer, always find out what
assortment of SIMM modules will be installed. If you
purchase an 8MB computer that has eight SIMM sockets on
the motherboard, the manufacturer will probably stuff a
1MB SIMM into each socket. That works fine, but leaves you
with no option but to throw away perfectly good SIMM
modules if you ever need to upgrade to 12MB or 16MB. It's
better to choose a computer that can be upgraded from
8MB to 16MB without throwing away SIMMs.

- The 386 and 486 computers have an additional type of memory on the motherboard called *external cache memory*. Consult your owners manual to find out if you can add additional cache memory using unused cache sockets. (The only benefit to increasing the amount of on-board cache memory is *speed*.)

- Older computers may us a more delicate type of memory chip called a SIP, whichstands for SIngle Inline Package. In a SIP, all of the pins protrude from one side of the chip. SIPs must be handled delicately to avoid bending or breaking the fragile pins.

Installing Motherboard Memory

If you need to install DIP chip memory on your computer's motherboard, follow these steps:

1. Gather your tools. At the minimum, you need medium- and small-sized Phillips and flathead screwdrivers. The best bet is to get one of those $15 assortments of computer tools, which includes all the right screwdrivers plus several other tools that might come in handy. A flashlight isn't a bad idea, either.

2. Turn off your computer and unplug it.

   Never work inside your computer with the power on or the power cord plugged in!

3. Clear an area around your computer where you can work. If the monitor is sitting on top of the computer, move it aside.

4. Remove the screws that hold the case. Usually, there are five or six screws at the back of the computer. (There are probably several other screws back there which you shouldn't disturb. Study it for a moment to determine which ones hold the case together.)

5. Gently slide the case off the computer. Usually, the case slides forward. You may have to lift and wriggle it a bit, but it should slide right off.

6. Touch the metal chassis to discharge any static electricity you may be carrying around.

7. Look around a moment to orient yourself. The motherboard is the big square or rectangular circuit board that everything else seems to be sitting on top of. Find the DIP sockets that the memory needs to be installed into.

8. Double-check the diagram in your owner's manual to make sure you've found the right sockets.

9. **DIP Chips:** DIP chips come in plastic tubes, nine to a tube. Slide the first chip out of the tube, and set it on top of the first empty socket so that the dot or groove at the top of the chip is lined up with the dot or groove on the socket. Look closely to make sure that each pin is lined up perfectly with its hole in the socket and then press the chip into place. Repeat for each chip.

   SIMM Modules: SIMM modules look like little mustache combs. To install a SIMM module into its socket, drop the business edge of the SIMM (the edge with the metal connectors) into the socket, laying the SIMM itself at a bit of an angle. Then tilt the SIMM back into place so that it snaps into the socket. This is harder to describe than to do. You don't have to worry about inserting the SIMM in backwards because there's only one way it can go.

10. Slide the case back onto the computer and reinsert the screws that you removed in step 4.

11. Plug the computer back in and turn it on.

12. If you get an error message informing you that the amount of memory installed doesn't match the "CMOS Configuration" or "Setup data," then run your computer's setup program and change the memory setting to the correct amount.

13. Put your tools away.

Adding a Memory Expansion Card

If you've installed one adapter card, you've installed them all. In other words, installing a memory expansion card is the same as installing a modem, a new display adapter, or a network card. If you've ever installed one of those cards, you can probably skip this procedure and install your memory expansion card blindfolded.

Before you begin this procedure, make sure that any DIP or SIMM memory is correctly installed on the card, and any switches or jumper blocks are properly set.

1. Collect the usual assortment of tools. You need medium- and small-sized Phillips and flathead screwdrivers. If you have one of those $15 computer tool kits, grab that. It has everything you need.

2. Turn off your computer and unplug it.

   Never work inside your computer with the power on or the power cord plugged in!

3. Clear an area around your computer where you can work. If the monitor is sitting on top of the computer, move it aside.

4. Remove the screws that hold the case. There should be five or six of them. Your computer probably has several other screws back there which you shouldn't disturb; stare at the back of your computer long enough to tell which is which.

5. Slide the case off the computer.

6. Touch the metal chassis to discharge any static electricity you may be carrying around.

7. Find an unused expansion slot inside the computer.

8. Remove the metal slot protector from the back of the computer's chassis. Save the screw.

9. Insert the memory expansion card into the slot. Line up the connectors on the bottom of the card with the connectors in the expansion slot, and then press the card straight down.

10. Secure the card with the screw you removed in step 8.

11. Slide the case back onto the computer and reinsert the screws that you removed in step 4.

12. Plug the computer back in and turn it on.

13. Clean up your mess.

Part VII

Jargon and Buzzwords

8-bit

A type of computer processing in which data is manipulated 8 bits at a time. An 8-bit number can represent 256 different values, and 8-bit bytes form the basis of modern computer memory storage (8 bits = 1 byte). The original IBM PC was built using an 8-bit data bus, which meant that data could be transferred to or from peripheral devices only 8 bits at a time. No IBM PC or compatible has ever utilized an 8-bit CPU, however.

16-bit

A type of computer processing in which data is manipulated 16 bits at a time. A 16-bit number can represent 64,384 different values. The CPU chip used in the original IBM PC — the 8088 — is a 16-bit processor, which means that data is moved in and out of the CPU 16 bits at a time.

The data bus on an IBM PC/AT used a 16-bit design, which meant that data could be transferred to and from peripheral devices 16 bits at a time. This same 16-bit bus design is used on most personal computers sold today; it's called the Industry Standard Architecture, or ISA, bus.

32-bit

A type of computer processing in which data is manipulated 32 bits at a time. A 32-bit number can represent more than 4 billion different values. The 80386, 486, and Pentium CPU chips are 32-bit designs, and most new computers come equipped with a *local bus* that transfers data 32-bits at a time.

32-bit CPUs also use 32-bit memory addresses, which means they are capable of accessing up to 4 billion bytes (GB) of memory. Most PCs sold today are limited to a maximum of 32 or 64MB of memory, though. At a typical cost of $50 per MB of memory, it would cost $204,800 to add 4GB to a computer. Given the rate at which computer memory needs have been increasing, however, it probably won't be too long before 4GB isn't enough memory. (I know you think I'm kidding....)

80286

An ancient ancestor to modern CPU chips which is unfortunately still used by far too many people. The 80286 chip was used in IBM's AT computers and in clones of the AT. It is a 16-bit processor that utilizes 24-bit addresses, which enable it to access as much as 16MB of memory.

The 80286 was the first CPU that was able to access extended memory. However, most of the memory management techniques described in this book are not possible on 80286-based computers. In particular, you cannot use EMM386.EXE on 80286 computers. That means you cannot load programs into upper memory or use extended memory to simulate expanded memory.

80287

The 80287 is a math coprocessor, a companion chip to the 80286 designed for intensive mathematics. Specifically, it provides instructions for floating-point math (math that involves decimals). By itself, the 80286 is capable only of integer math (math involving whole numbers). This doesn't mean you can't do fractions or decimal calculations on an 80286 computer that doesn't have a math coprocessor. However, programs that do intensive math (such as spreadsheet programs) operate much faster on computers that have floating-point math support.

80386

The CPU chip that replaced the 80286 as the first 32-bit micro processor. It has largely been replaced by the faster and more powerful 80486 and Pentium processors. A 386 processor is the baseline configuration for most of the memory management techniques presented in this book.

Intel also produced a 386SX chip. This CPU was functionally the same as the regular 386 chip but used a 16-bit data path instead of a 32-bit data path. In other words, the 386SX is a 32-bit processor in the inside, but to the outside world, it looks like a 16-bit processor. This allowed manufacturers to build inexpensive 386SX computers without having to create completely new motherboard designs.

80387

The math coprocessor companion chip for the 386 processor. A 386 computer that is equipped with a 387 coprocessor can run math-intensive programs such as spreadsheet programs faster than a computer that doesn't have the coprocessor.

80486

The most popular processor today. The 486 improves on the 80386 in several ways, the most important being that 80486 CPUs incorporate a math coprocessor in the chip. As a result, there is no separate 80487 math coprocessor to contend with. The 80486 chip is usually referred to as just a 486, or sometimes as an i486.

Just to confuse matters, Intel decided that the SX designation for the 80486 would mean something completely different than it did for the 80386. For the 80386, SX meant that the CPU had a 16-bit external data path even though it had a 32-bit internal design. For the 486, Intel changed the SX designation. It now means that the 486SX doesn't have a built-in math coprocessor. The 486SX is a full 32-bit CPU. (Okay, I lied. If you have a 486SX processor, you can get an 80487SX math coprocessor. But why would you? You'd save hundreds of dollars by buying a regular 486 processor in the first place.)

8086

A slightly more sophisticated cousin of the 8088, which featured a 16-bit data bus rather than an 8-bit bus. The 8086 was more powerful than the 8088, but the 8088 allowed manufacturers to build less expensive motherboards, so the 8086 never really caught on.

8088

The CPU around which the original IBM PC was built. The 8088 was a 16-bit processor that used a peculiar 20-bit addressing scheme which enabled it to access as much as 1MB of memory. Although the 8088 was a 16-bit processor, it used an 8-bit data bus.

A20 line

The A20 line is what makes the first 64K of extended memory available as the High Memory Area (HMA) on an 80286 or better processor. The HMA is possible because of a quirk in the original design of the 8088 CPU's segment:offset memory scheme. It would be fun to explain how it works here, but you'd probably send me a letter bomb.

Address

A number that uniquely identifies each byte of memory that can be accessed by the computer. The total amount of memory that a computer can support is limited by the number of binary digits used to formulate addresses. The 8088 processor used by the original IBM PC uses 20-bit addresses, which means that up to 1MB of memory can be accessed.

Wait a minute — isn't the 8088 a 16-bit processor? Indeed it is. To use 20-bit addresses, the designers of the 8088 use a twisted memory scheme known as segment:offset addressing in which two 16-bit numbers are added together to form a complete address.

Hold it again — wouldn't two 16-bit numbers give you a 32-bit number? Not the way Intel decided to do it. Intel drew an imaginary line at every 16 bytes of memory, dividing the entire 1MB memory space into 64,384 *segments*. The first part of an address is a 16-bit *segment address,* which identifies which of the 64,384 segments contains the byte of memory we're looking for. The second part is a 16-bit *offset,* which is added to the segment address to refer to a specific byte of memory.

Warning: Do not read the rest of this definition unless you understand hexadecimal numbers!

Segment:offset pairs are usually set off by a colon. Thus, 0100:0000 refers to segment 0100, offset 0000. The segment:offset addressing scheme has two interesting peculiarities. One is that any byte of memory can be represented by several different segment:offset pairs. For example, the byte at 0000:0050 could also be addressed as 0001:0040, 0002:0030, 0003:0020, or 0004,0000.

The second peculiarity is that the highest segment (FFFF) resides just 16 bytes below the 1MB memory limit. If you add an offset greater than 0010 (remember, we're talking hex here), you end up with an address that's beyond the 1MB limit. On an 8088 processor, the CPU automatically "wraps" such addresses back to the bottom of conventional memory. On an 80286 or better processor, however, such addresses can be used to access the first 64K of extended memory without leaving real mode. This quirk is the basis of how MS-DOS is able to access the High Memory Area (HMA).

Address space

The range of addresses that can be generated by a particular CPU, as determined by the number of bits used to form addresses. In real mode, addresses are constructed from a 20-bit segment:offset pair, so the address space is limited to 1MB. On an 80286, the address space is 16MB. On a 386 or better, the address space is 4GB.

ASCII

American Standard Code for Information Interchange, or something like that. A code that is used to represent letters, numerals, and symbols in computer memory and on storage devices such as disks and tapes. ASCII is simply a list of the letters, numerals, and symbols that correspond to each of the 256 different values that can be composed from an 8-bit byte.

AUTOEXEC.BAT

A batch file that is run automatically whenever MS-DOS starts.

Backfill

Expanded Memory Cards can be used on older 8088 or 80286 computers to fill in any conventional memory that is not installed on the motherboard using a technique known as *backfill*. Unless you're dealing with an older computer, you won't have to contend with backfill.

Bank

A *memory bank* is a group of sockets which must be filled with the same type of memory chips or SIMM modules. For example, my 486 computer has two banks of four SIMM sockets. That means that SIMM modules must be installed four at a time, using similar SIMM modules. You can't partially fill a bank, nor can you fill part of the bank with 1MB SIMMs and the other part with 4MB modules.

Bank switching

The technique used by EMS memory (expanded memory) to shuttle 16K portions of memory in and out of a 64K portion of memory known as the *page frame*.

BIOS

The Basic Input/Output System, a set of programs that are permanently stored in Read-Only Memory and enable the computer to communicate with I/O devices. The BIOS also maintains a small amount of battery-powered memory that keeps track of the computer's configuration.

Binary

The counting system used by computers. Unlike the decimal counting system, which utilizes 10 distinct numerals (0–9), the binary system uses only two numerals (0 and 1). This allows the computer to store information as sequences of electronic circuits which are either on or off.

You can blame binary for the fact that important computer numbers never seem to be properly rounded off. Why is one K actually 1,024 bytes? Why, oh, why is 1MB actually 1,048,576 bytes? Because of binary.

Bit

One binary digit, either a 0 or a 1. Bits are the building blocks of computer information.

Boot

The process of starting up your computer and loading MS-DOS into memory. Your computer boots itself whenever you turn it on, and you can reboot it by pressing the Ctrl, Alt, and Delete keys simultaneously.

Byte

A group of eight bits, the basic unit of information in personal computers. Using a code known as ASCII, one byte can be used to represent a single letter, numeral, or special character such as punctuation or other symbols.

Buffer

A 512-byte portion of memory that is used to hold data read from disk or waiting to be written to disk.

BUFFERS

A line in CONFIG.SYS that sets up buffers used for disk I/O. If a disk cache such as SMARTDRV is used, BUFFERS should be set to 10 or less to conserve memory.

Burr, Aaron

"I would not wish you to possess that kind of memory which retains with accuracy and certainty all names and dates. I never knew it to accompany much invention or fancy. It is almost the exclusive blessing of dullness." *Letter to his wife*, December, 1791.

Bus

The bacKone to which I/O devices such as disk drives, modems, and video displays are connected to the computer.

Cache

A sophisticated form of buffering in which a large amount of memory is set aside to hold data so that it can be accessed quickly. See *Disk cache*.

Carroll, Lewis

"It's a poor sort of memory that works only backwards," the Queen Remarked. *Alice's Adventures in Wonderland,* 1865.

CD-ROM

A high-capacity disk that uses optical technology to store data in a form that can be read but not written over. Two pieces of software must be loaded into memory to access a CD-ROM drive. First, a device driver that is supplied with the drive must be loaded by a DEVICE or DEVICEHIGH command in the CONFIG.SYS file. Second, the MSCDEX command must be included in the AUTOEXEC.BAT file.

CGA

An old-style color video monitor. CGA stands for Color Graphics Adapter, though by today's standards it should be called the Crayon Graphics Adapter.

CMOS

Complementary Metal Oxide Semiconductor, and it's a good thing because I'd hate to have to deal with *U*ncomplimentary *M*etal *O*xide *S*emiconductors. CMOS refers to the type of memory chips used for the battery-powered memory that keeps track of your computer's configuration and the date and time.

CONFIG.SYS

A file that contains special configuration commands which are processed when MS-DOS starts. The CONFIG.SYS file must reside in the root directory of drive C.

Configuration menu

A menu which is dispayed when MS-DOS boots. It allows you to select from several alternative start-up configurations. To create a configuration menu, you must include special commands in the CONFIG.SYS file to indicate what menu options should be displayed and what commands should be processed for each option.

Control Panel

A program supplied with Windows that allows you to configure various aspects of Windows and its operation.

Conventional memory

The first 640K of memory on your computer. In the early days when PCs were new, some computers had a puny 128K or 256K of conventional memory. However, selling a computer with less than 640K of conventional memory is a capital offense in most states.

The great goal of memory management is to make sure that as much of the 640K of conventional memory as possible is available for DOS-based application programs to utilize. With proper tuning, most computers can free up as much as 610K conventional memory for DOS program's use.

Conventional memory is the great equalizer. No matter how much memory your computer has, it can never have more than 640K of conventional memory. Even a memory show-off like my computer, with 20 whopping MB of memory, has but 640K of conventional memory. The excess memory beyond 640K is put to use as one of the other types of memory: upper memory, extended memory, or expanded memory.

CPU

The Central Processing Unit, or brains, of the computer.

Data

(1) The robot-Pinnochio character on *Star Trek: The Next Generation*. (2) Information processed by a computer.

DEVICE

The command you use in CONFIG.SYS to load a device driver.

Device driver

A special program that is loaded into memory via a DEVICE or DEVICEHIGH command in your CONFIG.SYS file and handles the petty details of accessing a hardware device such as a disk drive or a network adapter. Device drivers can be loaded into upper memory to preserve as much conventional memory space as possible.

DEVICEHIGH

The command you use in CONFIG.SYS to load a device driver into upper memory.

DIP

Dual Inline Package, a fancy term for "chip." Specifically, a DIP chip is a chip that has a row of pins protruding out and downward along two sides, making the chip look like something you would try to capture in a Roach Motel.

Disk cache

An area of extended or expanded memory that is used to hold data that would otherwise have to be read from or written to a disk drive. Because extended or expanded memory is much faster than disk storage, using a disk cache can make your computer run significantly faster. *Cache* is pronounced like *Cash*, which should be a $400 *Jeopardy* answer.

DMA Channel

DMA stands for Direct Memory Access; a DMA Channel is a special type of I/O connection in which an I/O adapter card is given direct access to the computer's memory.

DOS

Disk Operating System, the most popular operating system for IBM and IBM-compatible computers. Microsoft's version is known as MS-DOS; less popular versions, such as IBM's PC-DOS and Novell's Novell-DOS, are also available.

DoubleSpace

A feature of MS-DOS 6.0 and 6.2 which enables you to double the capacity of a hard disk by storing the data on the disk in a compressed form. Microsoft lost a patent lawsuit with a competitor shortly after MS-DOS 6.2 was released, so Microsoft was forced to replace DoubleSpace with a similar program called *DriveSpace* in MS-DOS 6.22.

Note that DoubleSpace does not increase the amount of memory your computer has — it compresses disk storage, not RAM.

DoubleSpace requires that a device driver (DBLSPACE.BIN) be present in conventional or upper memory; this device driver takes up 43K in MS-DOS 6.0 and 33–37K in MS-DOS 6.2. DBLSPACE.BIN is automatically loaded into memory when you start your computer, so you don't need to include a DEVICE command for it in your CONFIG.SYS file. However, the command **device=c:\dos\dblspace.sys /move** is required to move DBLSPACE.BIN into upper memory.

DPMI

DOS Protected Mode Interface, a set of rules developed by Microsoft that allows application programs to switch to protected mode and access extended memory on an 80286 or better computer.

DRAM

Dynamic Random Access Memory, inexpensive memory chips used for general-purpose memory. DRAM chips are called *dynamic* because they must be "recharged" periodically. Because of the recharge cycle, DRAM chips are a bit slower than their upscale cousins, SRAM chips. They're also considerably less expensive, which is why they are so popular.

DR-DOS

A DOS variant once sold by Digital Research, Inc., now known as Novell DOS.

DriveSpace

A feature of MS-DOS 6.22 which doubles the capacity of your hard disk be compressing information stored on the disk. DriveSpace is the successor to DoubleSpace, which was available with MS-DOS 6.0 and 6.2; it came about when Microsoft lost a patent infringement lawsuit filed by a competitor and was forced to pull DoubleSpace off the market. DriveSpace is in most respects identical to DoubleSpace.

Note that DriveSpace does not increase the amount of memory your computer has — it compresses disk storage, not RAM.

DriveSpace requires that a device driver (DRVSPACE.BIN) be present in conventional or upper memory; this device driver takes up 33–37K. DRVSPACE.BIN is automatically loaded into conventional memory when you start your computer, so you don't need to include a DEVICE command for it in your CONFIG.SYS file. However, the command **device=c:\dos\drvspace.sys /move** is required to move DRVSPACE.BIN into upper memory.

EGA

Enhanced Graphics Adapter, a color display standard that has been replaced by VGA.

EMM

See *Expanded Memory Manager.*

EMM386.EXE

An Expanded Memory Manager program that comes with MS-DOS Versions 5 and later and with Windows 3.1 and later versions. EMM386.EXE provides two basic functions: (1) it uses extended memory to simulate LIM 4.0 expanded memory, and (2) it serves as an Upper Memory Block (UMB) Provider. EMM386.EXE is loaded into memory using the command **device=c:\dos\emm386.exe**.

EMS

See *Expanded Memory Specification*.

ETLA

Extended Three Letter Acronym, which is actually a Four Letter Acronym. See *TLA*.

Expanded memory

A special type of memory that was used long ago to provide additional memory for 8088-type computers. True expanded memory resides on a special card that is inserted into one of the computer's expansion slots. However, 386 or better computers can use extended memory to simulate expanded memory. Expanded memory is also known as *EMM*, which stands for something you don't really need to know.

Expanded memory was used most often with older DOS-only versions of programs such as Lotus 1-2-3 or AutoCAD. Unless you use one of these programs, you have no need for expanded memory, either real or simulated. Note that the current versions of both these programs use more efficient extended memory instead, so you only need to use expanded memory if your boss has been too cheap to pop for a software upgrade in the past five years or so.

Expanded Memory Manager (EMM)

A device driver that implements expanded memory. The EMM may utilize extended memory to simulate expanded memory, or it may access memory on a memory expansion card. Either way, the EMM makes it possible for MS-DOS programs to use expanded memory.

Expanded Memory Specification (EMS)

A set of rules for accessing expanded memory. EMS is also known as the LIM specification, after the three companies that hashed it out: Lotus, Intel, and Microsoft. See *LIM EMS 4.0*.

Expansion bus

See *bus*.

Expansion card

An electronic card that can be plugged into one of the slots on the expansion bus. Memory expansion cards allow your computer to access additional expanded or extended memory.

Extended memory

Any memory beyond the first 1MB of memory on an 80286 or later computer. If you buy a computer with 4MB of memory, you get 3MB of extended memory. My computer with 20MB of memory has 19MB of extended memory.

For extended memory to be usable by DOS or Windows, it must be converted to *XMS memory* by a handy program called HIMEM.SYS (*XMS* stands for *Extended Memory Specification*, but that won't be on the test). Fortunately, HIMEM.SYS comes with MS-DOS 5 and 6 and Windows 3.1. Just make sure the following line is inserted in your CONFIG.SYS file:

```
device=c:\dos\himem.sys
```

You can insert this line in CONFIG.SYS yourself, or you can let the MemMaker command do it for you automatically.

Extended Memory Specification (XMS)

A set of rules for accessing extended memory. MS-DOS 5.0 and later and Windows 3.1 and later come with HIMEM.SYS, a device driver that manages XMS memory.

FCB

File Control Block.

File

A collection of information stored on disk. Disk storage, not memory, is used for permanent file storage. However, the contents of a file such as a document or a spreadsheet can be loaded into memory so you can work with it with an application program. After you work with a file in memory, it is important to use the application program's Save command to save any changes you make to the file back to disk.

File Control Block (FCB)

Version 1.0 of MS-DOS required one File Control Block (FCB) for each file it could open simultaneously. Each FCB requires 60 bytes of conventional memory. File Control Blocks are considered obsolete, having been replaced years ago by more efficient File Handles. However, MS-DOS still uses FCBs to support old programs that don't know how to use file handles. FCBs are strictly internal to DOS and don't affect you at all, except that you can use the CONFIG.SYS FCB command to set the number of File Control Blocks MS-DOS uses.

File handle

An improved method for handling files that was first introduced with MS-DOS 2.0. MS-DOS uses one file handle for each file that can be opened simultaneously. You don't have to worry about file handles unless you get an error message indicating that there aren't enough handles available to open a file. Then you can use the CONFIG.SYS FILES command to increase the number of file handles used by MS-DOS. Each file handle requires 60 bytes of conventional memory.

GB

Gigabyte, roughly one billion bytes (1,024MB to be precise). Although a 386 or better computer is theoretically capable of supporting up to 4GB of RAM, the motherboard of such a computer would have to have 1,024 SIMM sockets to support that much memory using 4MB SIMM modules. So the term *Gigabyte* is rarely used to refer to RAM; it usually refers to disk storage instead. See *MB* and *K*.

Hexadecimal

Are you sure you want to know about this? Here we go then. Hexadecimal, or just *hex,* is a number system that uses base 16 rather than base 10. In base 16, you have to have 16 numerals: the digits 0 through 9, followed by the letters A for 10, B for 11, C for 12, D for 13, E for 14, and F for 15. Thus, the number 10 in hexadecimal is actually 16.

Hexadecimal would be nothing more than a cruel math teacher's joke were it not for the fact that it can be used as a shorthand for binary numbers, with each hexadecimal digit substituting for four binary digits. For example, the binary number 10110101 can be represented in hexadecimal as B5.

Whenever this or any other book refers to a memory address, you can assume it is speaking in hex. For example, in the segment:offset address A000:0100, the segment is hexadecimal A000 and the offset is hexadecimal 0100. Sometimes you'll see a little *h* after the number to remind you that it is a hex number, as in 0100h.

Hex can be a little daunting at first, but the key to getting comfortable with hex is not worrying about what the "real" number is. When you work with memory addresses, you don't need to convert from hex to decimal or vice versa. If you see that the segment address is FB00, think of it as FB00. Don't try to convert that to a decimal number.

High memory

The first 64K of extended memory, which can be used almost as if it were extra conventional memory by utilizing an advanced programming technique formally known as "smoke and mirrors." Smoke and mirrors works only on 386 or better computers. The 64K in question is often referred to as the *High Memory Area*, or *HMA*.

Believe it or not, the preceding wisecrack about "smoke and mirrors" is a technically accurate description of how MS-DOS is able to seize 64K of extended memory and pretend it's extra conventional memory. You don't really want to know how it works. Trust me. (Okay, if you *really* want to know, look up *A20 Line*.)

HIMEM.SYS

An XMS extended memory manager provided with MS-DOS 5.0 and later as well as Windows 3.1 and later. HIMEM.SYS allows MS-DOS programs to access extended memory using the XMS standard. It also enables access to the High Memory Area (HMA). HIMEM.SYS is activated by a **device=c:\dos\himem.sys** command in the CONFIG.SYS file.

HMA

High Memory Area. See *High memory*.

i486

A trendy name for the Intel 80486 chip.

Intel

The company that designs and manufactures the CPU chips that power IBM-compatible personal computers. Well, most of them anyway. In recent years, several chip manufacturers have begun to copy Intel CPU designs. Intel still has an overwhelming share of the CPU market, however.

Map **201**

IRQ

Interrupt ReQuest. The mechanism used by I/O devices to signal the CPU that they need immediate attention. Fifteen different IRQs which must be assigned to the various I/O devices connected to the computer are available . One of the most difficult aspects of installing a new hardware adapter card is assigning it an IRQ that isn't already being used by another device.

ISA

Industry Standard Architecture, the name used to describe the expansion bus used on most computers. See *Bus*.

K

Kilobytes, roughly one thousand bytes (1,024 to be precise). See *GB* and *MB*.

LIM EMS 4.0

Lotus Intel Microsoft Expanded Memory Specification, Version 4.0. This is the latest incarnation of this specification, which is used by most MS-DOS programs that utilize expanded memory.

Load

A verb used to describe the process of reading a computer program's instructions into RAM memory and executing the program. Most programs are unloaded (removed) from memory after they finish executing, but two types of programs remain in memory until you reboot your computer: memory-resident programs and device drivers.

LOADHIGH (LH)

An MS-DOS command that loads a program into upper memory.

Low memory

Another term for conventional memory. The term is also sometimes used to refer to the first 64K of conventional memory.

Map

No memory management book would be complete without a *memory map*, which is a graphic representation of how memory is used. Memory maps are free to AAA members.

Here is a typical memory map that shows how conventional memory, upper memory, the high memory area (HMA), and Extended memory are laid out on a computer with 4MB of RAM:

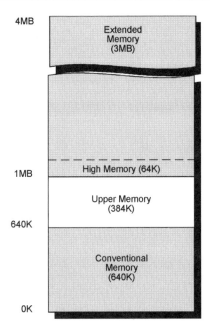

The following map shows the detail of how the upper memory area is utilized. From this map you can see that the amount of memory that is free in the upper memory area depends on what type of hardware your computer uses but that large portions of the upper memory area fall in the "unused" category.

MB

Megabytes, or roughly one million bytes (1,024K to be precise).
The amount of RAM installed in most computers is measured in
megabytes. See *GB* and *K*.

MDA

Monochrome Display Adapter, the original display adapter for the
IBM PC.

MemMaker

A program provided with MS-DOS 6 that automatically organizes
your upper memory as efficiently as possible.

Memory

An electronic device that is capable of storing and retrieving
information. Memory is used by the CPU to hold programs as
they execute and the data being manipulated by the programs.
See *RAM* and *ROM*.

Don't confuse computer memory (RAM or ROM) with disk
storage. Disk storage is a more permanent storage medium
designed for long-term storage. Memory and disk storage are
entirely separate beasts, and you can't solve a problem with one
by futzing with the other. For example, if you get a message that
says you don't have enough memory to run a program, deleting
files from your hard disk won't help free up any memory. Or, if
you get a message saying you have run out of disk space, running
MemMaker won't free up any disk space.

Memory-resident program

A program that remains in memory after it returns to the DOS
command prompt. The memory-resident program then remains
dormant in computer memory until some specific event, such as
accessing the disk or pressing a particular keyboard key, causes
it to come to life. Examples of memory-resident programs that
come with MS-DOS are SMARTDRV, PRINT, and VSAFE.

Memory-resident programs are often the source of memory
management troubles, for two reasons. First, they consume valuable
RAM, leaving less RAM available to run other programs. And second,
they sometimes conflict with one another or with application
programs, causing your computer to hang unexpectedly.

The LOADHIGH command can be used to force memory-resident
programs to load into upper memory.

Menu, Configuration

See *Configuration menu.*

Monochrome

A single-color display adapter. Monochrome monitors are usually green-on-black or amber-on-black, but some of the fancier ones used for desktop publishing purposes are black-on-white.

Motherboard

The main computer circuit board which holds the CPU, memory, sockets for expansion cards, and a handful of other chips.

MS-DOS

The official name of the DOS operating system from Microsoft. See *PC-DOS* and *DR-DOS.*

Multiple configuration

See *Configuration menu.*

Multitasking

The ability of a computer to run more than one program at once, much as a juggler can somehow keep five or six balls in the air at once.

There are two basic types of multitasking: nonpreemptive and preemptive. In nonpreemptive multitasking, each program that gets control of the computer holds on to control until it decides to let go. This is the way multitasking works in Windows 3.1. In preemptive multitasking, a supervisory program keeps tabs on how much time each program runs, intervening if necessary to let another program have a turn. This is the type of multitasking that will be provided by Windows 95.

Incidentally, multitasking is usually associated with 386 or better processors, but even the lowly 8088 CPUs supported a crude form of multitasking in the form of memory-resident programs.

Novell-DOS

An alternative version of DOS sold by Novell (formerly known as DR-DOS).

Offset

The second part of a segment:offset address. The offset is added to the segment to determine the actual address of a byte of memory. See *Address.*

Optimize

The process of configuring memory so that it is used as efficiently as possible.

Parity

A slick computer trick that helps your computer make sure its memory is operating correctly. A *parity bit* is added on to each byte of memory, so each byte is actually made up of 9 bits, not 8. Whenever data is written to a byte of memory, the computer hardware adds up the 8 bits that make up the byte. If the resulting number is even (that is, divisible by two), the parity bit is set to 1. Otherwise, it is set to 0. As a result, if all nine bits — the eight bits that make up the byte and the parity bit — are added together, the resulting number should be odd. If the result is even, a *parity error* has occurred and the byte of data at the memory location is not to be trusted.

PC-DOS

A mutant DOS version sold by IBM.

Pentium

The newest CPU chip from Intel, used in the sizzling hot computers that all of my friends seem to have.

Permanent swap file

See *Swap file*.

PIF

Program Information File, a special file that Windows can use to control the way MS-DOS programs are handled when run from within Windows.

PIF Editor

The program supplied with Windows to edit Program Information Files. The PIF Editor is found in the Main program group.

Processor

Another name for *CPU*.

Protected mode

One of the three major modes in which Intel CPUs operate, the other two being *real mode* and *V86 mode*. Protected mode allows the processor to access extended memory and provides advanced features for multitasking. Protected mode is available only on 80286 or later processors.

PSF

Permanent Swap File. See *Swap file*.

RAM

Random Access Memory, your comptuer's main memory. See *memory*.

RAM drive

A simulated disk drive that uses extended or expanded memory instead of actual disk storage. Because RAM memory is much faster than disk storage, data can be read to and written to a RAM drive much faster than a real disk drive. However, any data in a RAM drive is permanently lost when you turn your computer off or reboot it. As a result, critical information such as data files should not be stored on a RAM drive.

Real memory

The genuine article, as opposed to fake memory, which is more properly called *virtual memory*. Real memory refers to the RAM chips that are actually installed in the computer. See *Virtual memory*.

Real mode

One of three processing modes for Intel CPUs, the other two being *protected mode* and *V86 mode*. In real mode, 80286, 386, 486, or Pentium processors operate as if they were very fast 8088 processors. In other words, real mode is the mode of the original 8088 CPU. Real mode is a necessary evil; without it, you wouldn't be able to run programs written for an 8088-based computer on an 80286 or better CPU.

MS-DOS is a real-mode operating system, but interestingly, most uses of 386 or better processors don't run MS-DOS in real mode. Instead, they run it in V86 mode under the control of EMM386.EXE. See *V86 mode* if you're crazy enough to care about the distinction.

Resource heaps

See *System resources*.

ROM

Read-Only Memory. Memory chips which can be read but not written and retain their contents even after power has been turned off. The computer's BIOS is stored in ROM, which is why it is sometimes called the ROM BIOS.

Segment

The first part of a segment:offset address. The segment is multiplied by 16, and then added to the offset to determine which byte of memory to access.

Shadow RAM

ROM has the advantage of being permanent, but it also has the disadvantage of being slower than RAM. As a result, some computers have the ability to copy portions of their ROM BIOS instructions from ROM to RAM chips each time the computer starts. This enables BIOS instructions to run faster. However, it also steals away RAM chips that could be used for extended memory.

Shakespeare, William

"There's hope a great man's memory may outlive his life half a year." *Hamlet*.

SIMM

Single Inline Memory Module. An effective way of packing memory in which groups of nine chips are assembled onto a little card that looks like a mustache comb. SIMMs are readily available in 1MB and 4MB sizes.

SIP

Single Inline Package. A type of memory chip in which all the pins protrude from one end. Not used much any more.

SRAM

Static Random Access Memory, a breed of computer memory chips that are faster but more expensive than the more commonly used DRAM chips. SRAM chips are often used for external cache memory. See *DRAM*.

Stack

Intel processors provide a special method of storing and retrieving information in RAM called a Stack. The stack works like a stack of plates: the only way to add something to the stack is to put it on the top, and the only way to remove an item is to take the top one off the stack.

The stack is crucial to the correct operation of MS-DOS. If MS-DOS runs out of stack space, your computer will probably lock up, or you'll get a message about not having enough stack space. You can use the CONFIG.SYS STACKS command to increase the amount of RAM space dedicated to the stack.

Storage

The term storage is usually used to refer to disk storage, not RAM or other types of computer memory. It is very important that you understand the difference between disk storage and memory.

Memory, sometimes called *RAM*, is used by the CPU to hold programs as they execute and the data being manipulated by the programs. Disk storage is a more permanent storage medium designed for long term storage. Memory and disk storage are entirely separate beasts, and you can't solve a problem with one by futzing with the other. For example, if you get a message that says you don't have enough memory to run a program, deleting files from your hard disk won't help up any memory. Or, if you get a message saying you have run out of disk space, running MemMaker won't free up any disk space.

Super VGA

A display adapter that is compatible with VGA adapters, plus provides additional bells and whistles.

Swap file

A disk file that Windows uses as an extension of real memory. The swap file can be temporary or permanent. A permanent swap file is more efficient than a temporary swap file, but consumes valuable disk space.

System Resources

Although Windows lets programs access mass quantities of extended memory, it is still constrained by the segment:offset addressing scheme used by Intel processors. One of the most troubling by-products of this addressing scheme is that Windows stores critical information about executing programs in special areas of memory called *resource heaps*, which can be no larger than 64K. When these resource heaps fill up (and they do suprisingly quickly), Windows starts complaining that it is running out of memory.

You can determine how much free space remains in the resource heaps by using the Help⇨About command in Program Manager.

Three Finger Salute (TFS)

The technical term for rebooting your computer by pressing Ctrl, Alt, and Delete.

TLA

Three Letter Acronym. See *ETLA*.

TSR

A fancy term for a memory-resident program. *TSR* stands for *T*erminate and *S*tay *R*esident, which is the name of the MS-DOS routine that memory-resident programs use to establish their foothold in memory.

UMB

Upper Memory Block, an area of upper memory that can be used by programs or device drivers.

UMB provider

The program that doles out upper memory blocks. EMM386.EXE is the UMB provider that comes with MS-DOS 5 and 6 and Windows 3.1.

Upper memory

A 384K area of memory that follows immediately after the 640K of conventional memory. On a 386 or better computer, the unused portions of upper memory (called Upper Memory Blocks, or UMBs) can be used to hold programs that would otherwise consume conventional memory. This leaves more conventional memory available for DOS application programs. In MS-DOS 5, about 90K of upper memory can be used in this way. In MS-DOS 6, 155K of upper memory can typically be accessed.

The 8088 and 80286 computers have upper memory too, but they don't have the CPU horsepower to put it to any use other than what it was originally intended for. You must have a 386 or better computer to use upper memory to increase the amount of conventional memory available to your programs.

Upper memory is enabled by placing the following lines in your CONFIG.SYS file:

```
device=c:\dos\himem.sys
device=c:\dos\emm386.exe
dos=umb
```

You can place these commands in CONFIG.SYS yourself, or you can let the gentle MemMaker command do the work for you. Not only will MemMaker activate upper memory for you, but it will also automatically configure your computer to make the best possible use of upper memory.

V86 mode

One of three processing modes for Intel 386 and better CPUs, the other two being *protected mode* and *real mode*. V86 mode can be thought of as a protected-mode version of real- mode. It allows programs which were intended for real mode to be run in a multitasking environment under the control of a "hypervisor" program that runs in protected mode. If the hypervisor program is sophisticated enough, it can run more than one V86-mode program at once. These V86-mode programs are protected from one another so that if one of them freezes up, the others aren't affected.

The MS-DOS EMM386.EXE program is an example of how V86 mode can be used. EMM386.EXE acts as a "hypervisor" program controlling a single session of MS-DOS running in V86 mode.

VCPI

Virtual Control Program Interface, a set of rules developed by Phar Lap Systems that allows MS-DOS programs to switch to protected mode on 386 or better machines so they can access extended memory. See *DPMI*.

VGA

Video Graphics Array, the current standard in display adapters. Don't run Windows without it.

Video memory

The area of upper memory that is used by the video display adapter to hold the data that is displayed on-screen.

Virtual memory

Memory that isn't really there. Windows, by virtue of its swap file, is able to pretend that it has more RAM available to it than is actually present on the computer. See *Swap file*.

Virus

An evil computer program that sneaks into your hard disk and sometimes tries to destroy your files.

Wallpaper

A pattern or picture that is displayed in the background of the Windows desktop. It's pretty, but it consumes valuable system resources.

Windows

An operating system that makes DOS computers easier to use by letting the users click pretty pictures instead of making them type complicated commands. Windows allows programs to make free use of extended memory so they are not constrained by the 640K limit inherent with DOS, and it provides a limited form of multitasking. The current version of Windows is 3.11.

Windows 95

The much-anticipated replacement for Windows 3.1, which for the first time will not require MS-DOS as a separate entity on the computer. Windows 95 provides more advanced multitasking capabilities and more efficient memory management.

Windows for Workgroups (WfWG)

A networking version of Windows. WfWG Version 3.11 provides improved disk performance that is almost worth the price of the upgrade even without the networking features, and you don't *have* to have a network to use WfWG.

XMS

Microsoft's own set of rules for accessing extended memory. Once the HIMEM.SYS device driver has been loaded, extended memory becomes XMS memory, which can then be used by programs such as EMM386.EXE, SMARTDRV.EXE, and, of course, Windows.

Index

Notes

The fun & easy way to learn about computers and more!

Windows 3.1 For Dummies,™ 2nd Edition
by Andy Rathbone

1-56884-182-5
$16.95 USA/$22.95 Canada

The Internet For Dummies,™ 2nd Edition
by John R. Levine & Carol Baroudi

1-56884-222-8
$19.95 USA/$26.99 Canada

DOS For Dummies,® 2nd Edition
by Dan Gookin

1-878058-75-4
$16.95 USA/$21.95 Canada

Personal Finance For Dummies™
by Eric Tyson

1-56884-150-7
$16.95 USA/$21.95 Canada

PCs For Dummies,™ 2nd Edition
by Dan Gookin & Andy Rathbone

1-56884-078-0
$16.95 USA/$21.95 Canada

MORE Windows For Dummies,™
by Andy Rathbone

1-56884-048-9
$19.95 USA/$26.95 Canada

Macs For Dummies,® 2nd Edition
by David Pogue

1-56884-051-9
$19.95 USA/$26.95 Canada

WordPerfect For Windows For Dummies™
by Margaret Levine & David C. Kay

1-56884-032-2
$16.95 USA/$21.95 Canada

Over 12 Million in print!

Here's a complete listing of IDG's ...For Dummies Titles

Title	Author	ISBN	Price
DATABASE			
Access 2 For Dummies™	by Scott Palmer	1-56884-090-X	$19.95 USA/$26.95 Canada
Access Programming For Dummies™	by Rob Krumm	1-56884-091-8	$19.95 USA/$26.95 Canada
Approach 3 For Windows For Dummies™	by Doug Lowe	1-56884-233-3	$19.99 USA/$26.99 Canada
dBASE For DOS For Dummies™	by Scott Palmer & Michael Stabler	1-56884-188-4	$19.95 USA/$26.95 Canada

11/11/94

Title	Author	ISBN	Price
DATABASE (continued)			
dBASE For Windows For Dummies™	by Scott Palmer	1-56884-179-5	$19.95 USA/$26.95 Canada
dBASE 5 For Windows Programming For Dummies™	by Ted Coombs & Jason Coombs	1-56884-215-5	$19.99 USA/$26.99 Canada
FoxPro 2.6 For Windows For Dummies™	by John Kaufeld	1-56884-187-6	$19.95 USA/$26.95 Canada
Paradox 5 For Windows For Dummies™	by John Kaufeld	1-56884-185-X	$19.95 USA/$26.95 Canada
DESKTOP PUBLISHING / ILLUSTRATION / GRAPHICS			
CorelDRAW! 5 For Dummies™	by Deke McClelland	1-56884-157-4	$19.95 USA/$26.95 Canada
CorelDRAW! For Dummies™	by Deke McClelland	1-56884-042-X	$19.95 USA/$26.95 Canada
Harvard Graphics 2 For Windows For Dummies™	by Roger C. Parker	1-56884-092-6	$19.95 USA/$26.95 Canada
PageMaker 5 For Macs For Dummies™	by Galen Gruman	1-56884-178-7	$19.95 USA/$26.95 Canada
PageMaker 5 For Windows For Dummies™	by Deke McClelland & Galen Gruman	1-56884-160-4	$19.95 USA/$26.95 Canada
QuarkXPress 3.3 For Dummies™	by Galen Gruman & Barbara Assadi	1-56884-217-1	$19.99 USA/$26.99 Canada
FINANCE / PERSONAL FINANCE / TEST TAKING REFERENCE			
QuickBooks 3 For Dummies™	by Stephen L. Nelson	1-56884-227-9	$19.99 USA/$26.99 Canada
Quicken 8 For DOS For Dummies™, 2nd Edition	by Stephen L. Nelson	1-56884-210-4	$19.95 USA/$26.95 Canada
Quicken 5 For Macs For Dummies™	by Stephen L. Nelson	1-56884-211-2	$19.95 USA/$26.95 Canada
Quicken 4 For Windows For Dummies™, 2nd Edition	by Stephen L. Nelson	1-56884-209-0	$19.95 USA/$26.95 Canada
The SAT I For Dummies™	by Suzee Vlk	1-56884-213-9	$14.95 USA/$20.99 Canada
GROUPWARE / INTEGRATED			
Lotus Notes 3/3.1 For Dummies™	by Paul Freeland & Stephen Londergan	1-56884-212-0$	$19.95 USA/$26.95 Canada
Microsoft Office 4 For Windows For Dummies™	by Roger C. Parker	1-56884-183-3	$19.95 USA/$26.95 Canada
Microsoft Works 3 For Windows For Dummies™	by David C. Kay	1-56884-214-7	$19.99 USA/$26.99 Canada
INTERNET / COMMUNICATIONS / NETWORKING			
CompuServe Starter Kits For Dummies™	by Wallace Wang	1-56884-181-7	$19.95 USA/$26.95 Canada
Modems For Dummies™, 2nd Edition	by Tina Rathbone	1-56884-223-6	$19.99 USA/$26.99 Canada
Modems For Dummies™	by Tina Rathbone	1-56884-001-2	$19.95 USA/$26.95 Canada
MORE Internet For Dummies™	by John R. Levine & Margaret L.Young	1-56884-164-7	$19.95 USA/$26.95 Canada
NetWare For Dummies™	by Ed Tittel & Deni Connor	1-56884-003-9	$19.95 USA/$26.95 Canada
Networking For Dummies™	by Doug Lowe	1-56884-079-9	$19.95 USA/$26.95 Canada
ProComm Plus 2 For Windows For Dummies™	by Wallace Wang	1-56884-219-8	$19.99 USA/$26.99 Canada

11/11/94

11/11/94

Title	Author	ISBN	Price

PRESENTATION / AUTOCAD / PROGRAMMING (continued)

Title	Author	ISBN	Price
C For Dummies™	by Dan Gookin	1-878058-78-9	$19.95 USA/$26.95 Canada
C++ For Dummies™	by Stephen R. Davis	1-56884-163-9	$19.95 USA/$26.95 Canada
Mac Programming For Dummies™	by Dan Parks Sydow	1-56884-173-6	$19.95 USA/$26.95 Canada
QBasic Programming For Dummies™	by Douglas Hergert	1-56884-093-4	$19.95 USA/$26.95 Canada
Visual Basic "X" For Dummies™, 2nd Edition	by Wallace Wang	1-56884-230-9	$19.99 USA/$26.99 Canada
Visual Basic 3 For Dummies™	by Wallace Wang	1-56884-076-4	$19.95 USA/$26.95 Canada

SPREADSHEET

Title	Author	ISBN	Price
1-2-3 For Dummies™	by Greg Harvey	1-878058-60-6	$16.95 USA/$21.95 Canada
1-2-3 For Windows 5 For Dummies™, 2nd Edition	by John Walkenbach	1-56884-216-3	$16.95 USA/$21.95 Canada
1-2-3 For Windows For Dummies™	by John Walkenbach	1-56884-052-7	$16.95 USA/$21.95 Canada
Excel 5 For Macs For Dummies™	by Greg Harvey	1-56884-186-8	$19.95 USA/$26.95 Canada
Excel For Dummies™, 2nd Edition	by Greg Harvey	1-56884-050-0	$16.95 USA/$21.95 Canada
MORE Excel 5 For Windows For Dummies™	by Greg Harvey	1-56884-207-4	$19.95 USA/$26.95 Canada
Quattro Pro 6 For Windows For Dummies™	by John Walkenbach	1-56884-174-4	$19.95 USA/$26.95 Canada
Quattro Pro For DOS For Dummies™	by John Walkenbach	1-56884-023-3	$16.95 USA/$21.95 Canada

UTILITIES

Title	Author	ISBN	Price
Norton Utilities 8 For Dummies™	by Beth Slick	1-56884-166-3	$19.95 USA/$26.95 Canada

VCRs / CAMCORDERS

Title	Author	ISBN	Price
VCRs & Camcorders For Dummies™	by Andy Rathbone & Gordon McComb	1-56884-229-5	$14.99 USA/$20.99 Canada

WORD PROCESSING

Title	Author	ISBN	Price
Ami Pro For Dummies™	by Jim Meade	1-56884-049-7	$19.95 USA/$26.95 Canada
MORE Word For Windows 6 For Dummies™	by Doug Lowe	1-56884-165-5	$19.95 USA/$26.95 Canada
MORE WordPerfect 6 For Windows For Dummies™	by Margaret Levine Young & David C. Kay	1-56884-206-6	$19.95 USA/$26.95 Canada
MORE WordPerfect 6 For DOS For Dummies™	by Wallace Wang, edited by Dan Gookin	1-56884-047-0	$19.95 USA/$26.95 Canada
S.O.S. For WordPerfect™	by Katherine Murray	1-56884-053-5	$12.95 USA/$16.95 Canada
Word 6 For Macs For Dummies™	by Dan Gookin	1-56884-190-6	$19.95 USA/$26.95 Canada
Word For Windows 6 For Dummies™	by Dan Gookin	1-56884-075-6	$16.95 USA/$21.95 Canada
Word For Windows For Dummies™	by Dan Gookin	1-878058-86-X	$16.95 USA/$21.95 Canada
WordPerfect 6 For Dummies™	by Dan Gookin	1-878058-77-0	$16.95 USA/$21.95 Canada
WordPerfect For Dummies™	by Dan Gookin	1-878058-52-5	$16.95 USA/$21.95 Canada
WordPerfect For Windows For Dummies™	by Margaret Levine Young & David C. Kay	1-56884-032-2	$16.95 USA/$21.95 Canada

11/11/94

Qty	ISBN	Title	Price	Total

Shipping & Handling Charges

	Description	First book	Each additional book	Total
Domestic	Normal	$4.50	$1.50	$
	Two Day Air	$8.50	$2.50	$
	Overnight	$18.00	$3.00	$
International	Surface	$8.00	$8.00	$
	Airmail	$16.00	$16.00	$
	DHL Air	$17.00	$17.00	$

Please send this
order form to:
IDG Books
7260 Shadeland Station
Suite 100
Indianapolis, IN 46256

Allow up to 3 weeks for
delivery. Thank you!

Ship to:

Name _____

Company _____

Address _____

City/State/Zip _____

Daytime Phone_____

Payment:

☐ Check to IDG Books
   (US Funds Only)

☐ VISA

☐ MasterCard

☐ American Express

Card #_____

Exp. _____

Sign. _____

Subtotal _____

CA residents add
applicable sales tax_____

IN, MA, and MD residents
add 5% sales tax_____

IL residents add
6.25% sales tax_____

RI residents add
7% sales tax_____

TX residents add
8.25% sales tax_____

Shipping_____

Total_____

11/11/94

❏ YES!

Please keep me informed about IDG's World of Computer Knowledge. Send me the latest IDG Books catalog.